Make Me A Sabbath Of Your Heart

A Journey Into Living Like God

by

David M. Knight

Dimension Books
Denville, New Jersey 07834

248

ACKNOWLEDGEMENTS

I wish to express sincere thanks to Sister Marguerite John of the Monastery of St. Clare in Memphis for typing this manuscript, and to all of the Poor Clares for their prayer, encouragement and support; especially to Sister Helen Kelley, Abbess, and to Sister Peter Rowland and Sister Agnes Stretz, who are now founding a new Poor Clare monastery in Huehuetenango, Guatemala. Sister Agnes typed the first part of this manuscript before she left for Guatemala.

TABLE OF CONTENTS

CHAPTER ONE

BE MY GOOD NEWS ON EARTH
A Call To Be Different

Christian discipleship is a journey into living like God. Like every journey, it takes people away from where they are and leads them to something different. When everything remains the same, it is a sign that one is not moving. So when we look into discipleship, we have to ask ourselves, "What is different about being Christian?" What did Jesus teach that calls us to be so radically different from others? That is the theme of this book.

Before we ask what is different about being a Christian, however, we should first ask why we expect Christians to be different. After all, Christians follow a God who came *into* this world, not a God who stayed aloof from it. Jesus made Himself a part of human society. He belonged to a family, to a culture, to a people with definite ethnic characteristics; and He never repudiated any of this. He declared Himself free to renew and to transform His people and His world, but He did it from within, as one who remained a member, who continued to belong.

Jesus was a Jew. He thought and spoke and acted like a Jew. In fact, He was a small-town Jew, a country boy, and people thought of Him as such (*John* 1:46). He was also a member of a particular social class, and He was identified in the minds of those who knew Him with a particular working-class milieu. He was "the carpenter's son" (*Matthew* 13:55).

When Jesus was a child He played the games that children play (see *Matthew* 11:16-17). And when He was an adult He ate and drank like ordinary men, even though some found this a scandal in one whom they took to be a prophet and a guru (*Matthew* 11:19). Jesus didn't eat locusts and dress in camel's hair like John the Baptizer (*Matthew* 3:4). He enjoyed taking dinner with His friends (*Matthew* 26:6; *John* 12:2). He wept at funerals (*John* 11:35) and provided wine for a wedding reception (*John* 2:1 ff.). He didn't tell people to disown government and stop paying taxes (*Matthew* 22:21). On the contrary, He paid His own dues even when He wasn't obliged to (*Matthew* 17:24 ff.). He was caught up in family tensions just like everybody else (see *Mark* 3:21 and *John* 7:1-10) and, yes, He even had to cope with the characteristic oversolicitude of a Jewish mother! (*Matthew* 13:46-50)

Obviously, to follow Jesus one doesn't have to drop out of society, move to the mountains, form a separatist Christian commune, or renounce all family, social and cultural ties. In fact, the more one's religion seems to make one incapable of handling the ordinary relationships of family and social life, of business and civic involvement, the more suspect — from a Christian point of view — one's religion appears. Christianity is before all else an "incarnational" religion; that is, it is the word, the truth, the love of God *embodied* in the day-to-day activities and affairs of men. Jesus came to be in the world, to dwell in it, to interact with it and transform it; not to simply declare human society a hopeless mess and withdraw from it as far as He could.[1]

At the same time, Jesus makes it clear to His followers that they will never be able to just conform uncritically to the attitudes and values of any human society. Christians will never completely "fit in." The reason for this is that Jesus Himself did not "fit in." He did not repudiate human society or His Jewish culture; He did not seek to separate Himself from the life and activities of His nation. But because He was not simply and exclusively of their world; because He held up to them more than they wanted to receive, His people rejected Him. He was, in fact, more Jewish than any of them, more devoted to His people's authentic traditions and institutions. Nevertheless, the leaders of society arrested Him and accused Him before the people as a traitor who threatened everything Israel held most dear (see *Matthew* 26:57-68). And Jesus warned His followers that the world would treat them in the same way (see *John* 15:18 ff.; 16:1-4).

To be a disciple of Jesus, then, means to be different from the world. It doesn't mean to reject human society or to separate oneself from its activities. It means to remain in society being different. And if one isn't different in the way one engages in business, participates in social life, conducts oneself at home and manages one's family, then it is hard to maintain with any credibility that one is really a disciple of Jesus Christ.

This is the very first issue Jesus raises in the Sermon on the Mount. He begins that sermon — which Matthew presents as the first formal instructions we have from Jesus as "Master of the Way" —

by announcing the reversal of our most fundamental assumptions about life: "Blessed are the poor . . . the sorrowing . . . the lowly . . . the persecuted . . . " Since we have developed this theme in a previous book, we will not comment on the beatitudes here.[2]

Jesus follows up the beatitudes, however, with the challenging statement: "You are the salt of the earth . . . You are the light of the world" (*Matthew* 5:13-14). He leaves no doubt about the fact that He expects His followers to have a transforming, enlightening impact on the world — to take a leadership role in the course of human development.

Salt has two effects. First, it is a preservative; it keeps meat from going bad. And Christians, if they are the "salt of the earth," should keep society from going bad. Christians should act as a check on society's natural acceleration toward the false gods of sex, power and violence. Christians should keep the light of truth shining against the darkness which tries to engulf it (see *John* 1:4-5). Those who believe in Jesus should hold on to His values — and by keeping their own course, keep society aware and conscious of them — while the culture slips into one skid after another.

Against the destructive prejudice of sociological trends, education is not much defense. We have seen over and over again in history how the educators themselves have been the greatest misleaders. Karl Marx was an intellectual; so was Nietzsche, and before them Emmanuel Kant, David Hume and Descartes, just to mention a few samples. The United States Supreme Court justices who made it legal to abort living babies from their mothers' wombs were all intellectuals. No prejudices are stronger than the prejudices that reign in the intellectual establishment.

Human beings are all pretty much alike, and the virtues of humility and tolerance are no more evident on the university campuses than they are in the domain of the bigoted backwoods preacher that the television industry loves to pull out of its bag of stereotypes and parade before us everytime religion comes into a scene. The only difference I can discern between the bigoted, dogmatic fundamentalist and the bigoted, dogmatic intellectual is that the intellectual is supported in his prejudice by other intellectuals, while the fundamentalist is supported in his by other fundamentalists.

Brains aren't the answer, because brains, more than half of the time, are the original source of the problem. It is not the educated and the intellectual people who preserve society from corruption (that idea itself is one of the prejudices of the intellectual establishment which no one within the establishment is allowed to question); it is those who are open to the Spirit of God. These are the "salt of the earth."

Nor is anti-intellectualism the answer, as if the God who made the human brain didn't know how to work through it. There are people and groups who positively turn away from learning — from biblical scholarship in particular — as if education were both corrupt and corrupting by its very nature. These are the people and groups who believe that, in order to be open to the Spirit of God, they must be closed to everything else. Their fundamentalism is a "chosen ignorance," which is all the less authentic as a religious stance the more arrogant and judgmental toward others it becomes.

The arrogance of these extreme fundamentalists is shown above all in a rejection of all religious thought, reflection and experience that has taken place before them or is taking place right now outside of their own circle of enthusiasm. Fundamentalists of this sort do not read the lives of the saints or the writings of the mystics. They have nothing to learn from parents, ministers or priests whose relationship with God is less dramatic than theirs — not because it is less real, but because it has passed from the enthusiastic naivete of the spiritual honeymoon into longterm fidelity and commitment. In particular, the experience and tradition of the established churches have no value for them. God's real enlightenment of the human race began, for them, when they themselves saw the light — or when the evangelist they admire received his "call" — and God has never said anything to anyone that is deeper or more extensive than the message they have heard in their hearts. They want to share their experience of Jesus with the world. It never occurs to them that the rest of the world might have an even deeper experience of Jesus to share with them — one that is more quiet, more settled, and more enduring than their own, simply because it is more mature.

The "salt of the earth" are the disciples. Those who preserve the world from corruption are neither the sophisticated intellectuals of cultured society nor the deliberately ignorant enthusiasts of the self-nourishing sects. Those who keep the world from veering off into darkness are the disciples who walk, not by their own light or the light of this world, but by the light of Christ. And this light shines, not primarily through one individual or another, but through the Christian community as such.

It is significant that when Jesus described His disciples He compared them first of all to salt — which only works when there are many grains together — and then to the light, not just of a single lamp, but of a "city set on a hill" (*Matthew* 5:14). And even the single lamp that is mentioned in the next verse is an image used to describe, not one individual, but the whole community of believers.

The truth which is the light of the world is the truth given, not to several individuals as such, who then form a community (a church) because they all see and believe the same thing. Rather, it is truth given to the community as a whole, and each individual shares in this truth by sharing in the life and light of the community. Discipleship is a matter of learning, not directly from Jesus alone (although this is also essential), and not primarily from any individual teacher (although particular people have a precious influence on our lives) but from the Christian community as such. And this community embraces the members of every space and time. It is not just the community of today, or of one's own national, ethnic, or cultural milieu. It is the community of believers which stretches from the beginning of Christianity until our own times, and extends from one end of the earth to the other — the "catholic" community in the truest sense of the word.

For this reason, anyone who would be a disciple of Jesus without at the same time placing himself respectfully before the experience and tradition that has grown in the Christian community from biblical times until now is simply deceiving himself. The Jesus we learn from is not just the Master who taught by word and example for a few short years in Israel. Nor is He just the Jesus who spoke so forcefully and unerringly in the original twelve apostles. He is the Jesus who has spoken in the Church and through the community of believers from Pentecost until now.

As the Letter to the Hebrews instructs us: "Remember your leaders who spoke the word of God to you; consider how their lives ended, and imitate their faith. Jesus Christ is the same yesterday, today, and forever" (*Hebrews* 13:7-8).

To ignore the writings of the saints, whose "lives ended" in eloquent testimony to their faith, is to turn a deaf ear to the voice of Jesus speaking over the past two thousand years. Anyone who does that, and claims to be listening seriously to Him today, does not know who Jesus is.

In order to be the salt of the earth (and the light of the world) and to preserve society from the corruption of darkness, Christians must remain disciples of their own tradition. Salt, as a matter of fact, takes centuries to form; it is mined out of the ages-old rock or processed out of the timeless sea. Salt doesn't spring up overnight, and neither does the community which is charged by Jesus to be the salt of the earth.

Salt has another function. It not only preserves; it brings out the taste of whatever food it is mixed with. And Christians, mixed into the life and activities of this world, should bring out the true taste of whatever is going on. A Christian way of doing business is a way which brings out the true nature and value of the business itself. A Christian family life is one that gives to the reality of family as such a heightened taste, which is the true taste of what "home" and "married love" and "sexuality" and "children" should mean. And Christian worship, when it is properly conducted and participated in with faith, should give to all who engage in it a representative taste of what religion is able to be.

The "salt of the earth" brings out the taste of the earth. Whether or not one's own life has this transforming, heightening effect on the milieu one lives and works and worships in is a test of discipleship.

Salt preserves and brings out taste. Christian discipleship performs these same functions wherever it exists in the world: it preserves society from veering off into corruption, and it lifts up all the activities of human life to the level of their true meaning and value. But this does not just automatically happen wherever there are people who go by the name of Christian. Jesus warned us that the salt can lose its flavor; it can go flat. Then it is "good for nothing but to be thrown out" (*Matthew* 5:13).

Salt has a third effect: it arouses thirst. Wherever there are disciples of Jesus, the people around them should begin to thirst for deeper experience of God. The effect of authentic discipleship is to increase thirst for that truth and those values which are not simply and exclusively of this world. This thirst is never completely satisfied until we see God face-to-face in heaven. Therefore true discipleship is always a dynamic element and source of growth on earth.

Not every Christian is a disciple. This title belongs only to those who themselves are filled (or being filled) with the flavor of Christ's word. It is not enough to be one of those thousands or millions of Christians who have simply had the word of God explained to them one or more times, who have believed it, accepted it, and been received into the Church, but who give no time to personal reflection and prayer over the words of the Scripture themselves.

A disciple is one who prays. And the prayer of a disciple is reflection on the word of God.

Since I have explained at length in another book what the prayer of discipleship is and how to engage in it, I will not develop this theme here.[3] Our focus in this chapter is simply the fact that Jesus calls us to discipleship in the very beginning of the Sermon on the Mount, and that being a disciple calls for more than just routine membership in a church. A disciple is one who matches the description St. Paul gives of himself:

> Thanks be to God, who unfailingly leads us on in Christ's triumphal train, and employs us to diffuse the fragrance of his knowledge everywhere! We are an aroma of Christ for God's sake, both among those who are being saved and those on the way to destruction . . .   (2 *Corinthians* 2:15)

To be an "aroma of Christ" in the world, we have to be filled ourselves with the fragrance of Christ. And this is the "fragrance of his knowledge." To be the salt of the earth; to be the light of the world; to be the "aroma of Christ" among men, the requirement is always the same: we must be filled with the "fragrance of the knowledge of God," the fragrance of His word abiding in our hearts: remembered, reflected upon, tasted, appreciated, embraced in desire and in decision. This is what it means to be a disciple.

And this is what is different about Christians: they bring a new taste, a new light, a new fragrance into their environment because of the word of God which they remember and carry in their hearts.

FOOTNOTE

[1] This is in no way a criticism of monastic life. Monasteries are not communes. The goal of monasticism is not withdrawal from the world in order to seek a healthier human existence apart from the corruption of society. Monastic withdrawal is not an act of escape but a declaration of emancipation. Its purpose is not to be *free from* impediments to authentic human living, but to be *free for* those exercises which foster a particular experience of the life of grace. The goal of monasticism is not a fuller, healthier experience of family and social life, of work and of community,

but an experience of life on a different level entirely. That is why *renunciation* — of marriage and family, of material comforts and wealth, of autonomous self-determination in this world — through the vows of poverty, celibacy and obedience is essential to monastic withdrawal. Monastic withdrawal pronounces no judgment whatsoever on the quality of life in ordinary human society; its goal is simply to proclaim and be present to the truth of faith that God has called us beyond this world to share in the transcendent life of God. It is *renunciation* of the world, and renunciation made precisely as an expression of this faith, which spells the difference between a monastery and a commune. For a more adequate explanation of this see my books *Cloud By Day — Fire By Night: The Religious Life as Passionate Response to God* (Dimension Books, 1980), and *Lift Up Your Eyes To The Mountain,* chapter seven: "The Desert and the City: Two Paths of Perfect Gift" (Dimension Books, 1981).

² See *First Steps In Christian Discipleship — The Experience of Accepting Jesus,* chapters eight to fourteen (Dimension Books, 1982).

³ See *His Way — An Everyday Plan For Following Jesus,* chapters three and four, and the guidebook for study and discussion that goes with it: *To Follow His Way — A Parish Renewal Program,* pp. 30-39: "Second Group Meeting: Am I A Disciple?" Both of these books are available through bookstores or through the publishers, St. Anthony Messenger Press, Cincinnati, Ohio.

CHAPTER ONE: BE MY GOOD NEWS ON EARTH —
Matthew 5:13-16

Summary:

1. Discipleship is a journey. It implies change and becoming different from what we were before, different from the world around us. The goal of the journey is thinking and living like God.

2. Discipleship does not mean or require dropping out of the world or forming a separatist society. To be "light" and "salt" in the world, Christians must be in society, transforming it from within. Jesus as "Master of the Way" does not lead us out of the world, but through it. Discipleship is an effort to follow Jesus — to live by His mind and heart, and to let Him live in us — in the ordinary activities and choices of daily life.

3. The disciple of Jesus should not expect to "fit in" completely with any human society. If we want to conform to the

attitudes, values and behavior of our peer group, we cannot conform our hearts and minds to Christ's. If being accepted by others has priority with us, we cannot embrace Jesus as our Teacher or aspire to live like God on earth.

4. Jesus expects His disciples to have an enlightening, transforming effect on the world, to take a leadership role. As "salt of the earth" they should do three things: first, they are to preserve the world from veering off into corruption. Secondly, they should bring out the taste of created values, respecting the nature and goal of all human activities, but lifting them up and enriching them with the light, love and higher destiny taught by Christ. Finally, they should excite thirst for the life of grace and union with God offered by Jesus Christ.

5. It takes many grains of salt to produce its effect, many lights to make a "city set on a hill." Discipleship takes place within the community of believers, which embraces the members of every space and time. The light of Christ is not only beamed into each individual heart direct from God; it also comes to us reflected from all the other believers. To "walk in the day" is to walk in light that is all around us. It is to walk in the light which is given to the Church as such, as a community.

Questions for prayer and discussion:

1. What decisions have I made in life which were a direct result of thinking about the teaching of Jesus Christ? Did these decisions make me different in any way from my peer group?

2. How have I been (or am I being) "salt" and "light" to those around me? Have I had a braking or correcting influence on false trends? Have I lifted up or transformed in any way through my faith the activities I engage in with others? Have I excited in anyone a thirst to know Christ better and follow Him more closely?

3. In what ways do I receive the light of Christ from the Christian community? What preserves my discipleship from the narrowness of one age, country or culture?

CHAPTER TWO

THE MEANING OF DISCIPLESHIP
Beyond My Laws, My Heart

Discipleship is a call to be different. The light we guide our conduct by must be so much clearer and brighter than the light of our culture, Jesus tells us, that it will make us the "salt of the earth" and the "light of the world." And this is a test of discipleship. Unless the witness of our behavior is so striking that it affects our environment like the "aroma of Christ," the "fragrance of the knowledge of God," we are not being for Jesus or for the world what we should be. "Your light must shine before men," He tells us, "so that they may see goodness in your acts" — a goodness so striking, so outstanding, that their spontaneous reaction (if they are open to God, at least) is to "give praise to your heavenly Father" (*Matthew* 5:16).

This is the fruit of discipleship. By this fruit we know it is real.

But what does Jesus teach us that will help us to bear this fruit? What, specifically, does He tell us to do?

The very first thing Jesus teaches us is not to ask that question.

The corruption of Judaism by the Pharisees came from their desire — so natural to us all — to boil religion down to a set of cut-and-dried obligations. The essence of Phariseeism is not hypocrisy but the attempt to tie God down to a contract. We want God to tell us, once and for all, in clear and unmistakable language, exactly what we have to do to fulfill our obligations to Him. And then we want Him to leave us alone.

That is what a contract does: it makes it possible for two people to stop dealing with one another. The dealing, the human and personal interaction, takes place while the terms of the contract are being worked out. Once they are agreed upon, the two people never have to talk to one another again — at least not with the risk of personal interaction, personal exposure, personal acts of decision. Once the contract is made, we don't have to worry any more about how much we dare ask of the other, or how much the other might ask of us. We don't have to worry about whether we will be able, or whether we will want, to respond. We know exactly what is asked of us. We have had the chance to size it up, weigh its possible difficulty, assess the resources we have which will enable us to measure up to what is asked, and come to a sense of security based on knowledge of the whole situation and confidence in our ability to handle it.

A contract puts us in control. We are no longer dealing with the unknown, or interacting with someone equal to ourselves (or superior, as God is) but simply with a set of obligations. Like a building contractor, we have our "plans and specifications" and we can get to work. We are on top of the situation, doing what we know we can do.

God doesn't deal like this. God isn't interested in contracts, but in covenants. In a contract the focus is on what one has agreed to do. In a covenant the focus is on what one has agreed to *be* for another. Contracts spell out obligations; covenants define relationships. In a contract the important word is *what.* In a covenant the important word is *who.* And God has made it quite clear throughout history that what we do is only important to Him in terms of who we are for Him, who He is for us, and who we become for each other. God only created the world so that people might become. And we become, we become the "who," the persons that we are, through acts of free response to Him.[1]

Jesus makes clear from the very beginning of the Sermon on the Mount that law observance is not what His religion is all about. His disciples must go beyond that. They must observe whatever laws there are, of course, for this is just plain morality. But discipleship is something different than keeping laws. Discipleship is a matter of taking on attitudes and values; it is an interior change of mind and heart and will.

"Do not think I have come to abolish the law and the prophets," Jesus says. "I have come, not to abolish them, but to fulfill them." But He goes on to say that observance of the law, even the minute, perfect observance that the Pharisees strained after, is not the path of His followers. "I tell you, unless your holiness surpasses that of the scribes and Pharisees you shall not enter the kingdom of God" (*Matthew* 5:17-20).

What must we do to let our holiness "surpass that of the scribes and Pharisees?" The answer is, "We must become disciples." The difference between law observance and discipleship is this: law observance aims at doing what the law says to do; discipleship aims at acquiring for oneself the attitudes, values and vision of the person who made the law. An obedient person looks at what the law points to. A disciple looks at where the law is coming from. The goal of simple obedience is to keep on God's good side; or, on a more loving level, to be pleasing to Him. The goal of discipleship is to be united to God, to be one with Him in mind and will and heart. Law observance aims at uprightness; discipleship aims at union.

That is why a religion of law observance is not a religion of growth. As long as uprightness, right behavior, is the goal, the most a religion can aim at is healing. When we sin, we fall below par. When we repent and strive to be virtuous, we get back to normal; that is, to full and perfect observance of the law. And therefore the only movement to be experienced in a religion of law observance is a movement from sin to repentance, from vice to virtue, from alienation to acceptance, from feeling bad about oneself to feeling secure in one's own good behavior.

People whose religion is on this level sometimes find themselves sinning out of a subconscious desire to experience God! The only experience they have had of Him is that of being forgiven; and so when they thirst for His touch they sin in order to receive it through forgiveness.

Or they keep repenting of their sins again and again and again in order to have a sense of moving toward God. What they really want is *union* with

God, and the path to this is discipleship. But since they don't know what discipleship is, and the closest thing to union with God that they have experienced is acceptance by Him in forgiveness, repentance is the only thing they know that gives them a feeling of approaching God. Therefore, if they are not going over their checklist of faults and observances for a feeling of reassurance, they will probably be seeking the experience of devotion through another round of repentance. This is the way a religion of law operates.

This is the attitude St. Paul was talking about when he wrote to the Philippians: "But those things I used to consider gain I have now reappraised as loss in the light of Christ." What he "used to consider gain" was not riches, honors, pleasures, and the disappointing delights of sin; it was *law observance*. Paul had a passion for feeling good about himself, and what gave him this sense of security was observing the law. This is what he came to "reappraise" in the light of his experience of Christ:

> But those things I used to consider gain I have now reappraised as loss in the light of Christ. I have come to rate all as loss in the light of the surpassing knowledge of my Lord Jesus Christ. For his sake I have forfeited everything; I have accounted all else rubbish so that Christ may be my wealth and I may be in him, not having any justice of my own based on observance of the law. The justice I possess is that which comes through faith in Christ. It has its origin in God and is based on faith. I wish to know Christ and the power flowing from his resurrection; likewise to know how to share in his sufferings by being formed into the pattern of his death.
>
> (*Philippians* 3:7-10)

What Paul is describing here is a conversion to discipleship. The desire that rules his life in this passage is desire to *know Christ*, to be united with His mind and heart even to the point of sharing in Christ's own desire to suffer and die for the redemption of the world. The "faith" Paul speaks about as being the source of his justification is not just the fact, or the moral act, of believing that what Jesus said was true. It is the living faith of seeing through Christ's eyes, understanding by Christ's mind (*Philippians* 2:5; *Romans* 12:2), choosing in the power of Christ's Spirit (*Philippians* 2:13; *Colossians* 1:29; 2 *Corinthians* 7:6), loving with the love of Christ's own heart (*Romans* 9:2; *Ephesians* 3:14-21). This is what discipleship is all about.

It is only discipleship that makes Christianity a religion of growth. And only disciples can understand what the saints and writers are talking about when they speak of such stages of spiritual development as the "seven mansions" of St. Teresa of Avila, the "dark nights" of St. John of the Cross, or the "three ways" — the purgative, illuminative and unitive levels — of everyone's progress toward God.[2]

The tragedy of this is not that people do not know where they are in terms of Christian perfection. A preoccupation with how much progress you have made can be an obstacle to growth. The tragedy is that people do not even know — in any clear or explicit way — that they ought to be growing at all! They don't know that what they are experiencing as "religion" may be nothing more than the skin of the orange: that they have never penetrated to the fruit beneath, never even tasted it. And so we have the phenomenon of Christians who ought to know better turning away from the deep waters of Jesus Christ to play in the frothy shallows of enthusiastic, fundamentalist sects, or abandoning Christianity entirely to seek enlightenment and spiritual transformation at the feet of some esoteric guru.

Two evils have my people done:
they have forsaken me,
the source of living waters;
They have dug themselves cisterns,
broken cisterns that hold no water.

(Jeremiah 2:13)

Jesus did not say, "Go, therefore, and make obedient law-observers of all the nations." What He said was, "Go, therefore, and make disciples of all the nations" (*Matthew* 28:19). This is what God is moving people to in their hearts; this is what He is preparing them for, both in and outside of the Church. If the Church, therefore, does not offer people discipleship, they will find a way to be disciples anyway. They will attach themselves to anyone who offers to be their teacher — anyone, that is, who gives any appearance of having experienced more of the spiritual life than is evident in the congregations and ministers of our churches.

The question of discipleship, however, is not just a pastoral concern of the clergy — something the Church's ministers should address themselves to and set themselves to provide. Discipleship is first of all an invitation to each individual heart. It takes place within the Church, of course, in union with other believers. The flavor of salt comes from many grains together; the "city set on a mountain," which cannot be hid, is a city whose brilliance comes from many lights. But no one can contribute to the light of the Church, or truly be enlightened by the light of Christ shining in the Church, unless he or she takes time in private to reflect deeply on the word of God. God speaks to the heart in silence. The word of God is proclaimed from the housetops, but it is absorbed in the seclusion of one's own room (see *Matthew* 6:6), or while one is driving to work, or lying awake at night, or sitting in an airport waiting for a plane.

The essential is not where one prays, or when, or how much time each week one gives to it (to put the accent here could be just another Phariseeism, a new clause in our "contract" with God), but just that one should *absorb* the word of God with one's heart. There are people who devote time "religiously" every day to prayer, but who are not disciples at all. This is because their real goal is to give the time, or make their daily quota of Scripture reading, or complete five decades of the rosary, or live up to some other commitment they have made to God or to themselves. This fidelity to some concrete way of praying is all well and good. It is even essential if we are going to be serious about prayer, since no human being ever does anything consistently without commitment, and commitments only become real when they descend to the concrete details of time and space. But it is not discipleship unless, in addition to the fidelity we insist on, we also insist in first place and above all on making God's word the interior word of our own hearts. We have to strive with our minds to understand what we read, and seek with our hearts to appreciate and feel what is said to us. We have to find ways through our choices to put it into practice. Then we are disciples, because then what we are striving for is identification with Christ: union with Him in mind and heart and will.

When we ask Jesus, then, "Lord, what shall I do?" (see *Acts* 2:37; 22:10), the answer will not be a list of concrete things. Jesus will tell us, "Repent" — that is, change your whole way of thinking about reality, about the world, your life in it, and about God — "and follow me. Be my disciple."

And this will be a journey into living like God.

FOOTNOTE

[1] For more development of these ideas see my books *Cloud By Day — Fire By Night,* Vol. I, ch. 9, pp. 155 ff. (Dimension Books, 1980) and *The Good News About Sex,* chapters one to three (St. Anthony Messenger Press, 1979).

[2] Unfortunately, Teresa and John were writing for contemplatives, and ordinary people leading active lives may find their explanations hard to follow. For a simple and practical presentation of Christianity as a way of growth that working people can follow, see my book *To Follow His Way,* (St. Anthony Messenger Press, 1980). See also *Lift Up Your Eyes to the Mountain* (Dimension Books, 1981), which traces the path of spiritual growth from acceptance of the world and of oneself (the "valley") through seeking knowledge of God (the "mountain top") to a committed path of perfection (the "desert" or the "city").

CHAPTER TWO: THE MEANING OF DISCIPLESHIP — *Matthew* 5:17-20

Summary:

1. Discipleship differs from law observance the way a covenant differs from a contract. Contracts focus on what one promises to do for another; the emphasis is on performance. Covenants focus on who one promises to be for another; the emphasis is on relationship.
2. Contracts are cut-and-dried; they eliminate the risk of the unknown; they give us a sense of being in control. A religion of law-observance is like this. Covenants are open-ended; they leave us dealing with each other as free, responding persons who never know what or how much might be asked next. This is discipleship; it is a way of growth.
3. A religion of law-observance looks at what the law points to and aims at doing what it says. Discipleship looks at where the law is coming from and aims at union of mind and heart with the person who made the law. Law observance aims at keeping on God's good side; its ceiling is moral uprightness. Discipleship aims at identification with God in love; it is a commitment to growth without limits. That is why the

holiness Christians aim at must go beyond that of the scribes and Pharisees (*Matthew* 5:20). The goal of discipleship is as far beyond law-observance as perfection is beyond par.

4. Discipleship takes place within a community of believers, but it calls for individual, personal reflection. The word of God is proclaimed in public, but it is absorbed in solitude. Without significant moments of private reflection and prayer, no one can go beyond the beginnings of discipleship.

Questions for prayer and discussion:

1. What is the difference between a contract and a covenant? Give examples. Is marriage primarily a contract or a covenant? Why? What do I do that makes my own relationship with Jesus Christ a covenant rather than a contract?

2. How does my own response to Christ go beyond the upright behavior aimed at by the scribes and Pharisees? Am I one who both "fulfills and teaches" His commands (see *Matthew* 5:19)? Whether one actually teaches or not, what more is required in a teacher in terms of understanding than simply carrying out what the law commands? By this standard, do I have what it takes to both fulfill and teach the new law of Jesus?

3. In my own religious attitudes and practice, do I aim more at doing what the law says, or at understanding the mind and heart of God which inspired the law? Are my sights set only on moral uprightness, at keeping within the law of God, or am I aiming at perfect union of mind and heart and will with Jesus Christ? What concrete acts do (or would) express my real intention to grow toward union with Christ?

4. How much time do I spend in personal, private reflection on God's word? What time could I set aside for this each day? Where would I have to go for the privacy to think about God's word without interruption?

CHAPTER THREE

BE HOLY BECAUSE I AM HOLY
The Law of Likeness to God

When Jesus calls us to the interior journey of discipleship, His first step is to tell us that our focus should not be on the law, but on the mind and heart of God which inspired the law. His second step is to take us through the Ten Commandments, reinterpreting each commandment in a way that reveals the personality of God. The commandments were given to be a law for human behavior. Jesus rewrites them as a law for divine behavior. In this way He makes them into a revelation of God; that is, of the law which governs God's own life. And this is a law of unconditional love.

In the process of doing this Jesus also announces — in a very subtle and implicit way — the good news of the Kingdom. And the good news is simply this, that with the coming of Jesus we are invited to a union with God that is beyond our wildest imagining. We are invited to share in the life of God. (This is what "grace" is: the favor of sharing in God's own life). By this sharing in God's life we share in His mind and heart: we share in God's own act of knowing, in God's own act of loving, in God's own act of living, and in the joy, the beatitude that God finds in living His life of love. And that is why the law of God's behavior must be the law of our own.

This is the mystery of our union with God — the mystery of grace, the mystery of the Kingdom. And it is a mystery beyond anything the men and women of Jesus' time had ever dreamed of or been prepared to dream of.

They were not yet ready to hear it.

And so Jesus begins by talking about what they were able to hear. He talks about the Commandments. He talks about law observance, punishment and reward. He takes people where they are and talks to them about the thoughts that are familiar to them. But in the process He lifts up the level of their thinking and redirects it. He gets them thinking — still unconsciously and implicitly — in terms of the grace of being one with God. He does this by changing the whole perspective from which they were used to looking at the law, at religion, at life on this earth and the prospect of life after death. He stands with them as they look at the law and He talks to them about the Commandments from the perspective of His own knowledge of the Kingdom and of God's heart. And as He does this He reveals to them in an implicit and still unrecognized way what the good news really is: it is the news of our call to share both now and forever in the life that is proper to God alone.

The first commandment Jesus comments on is Exodus 20:13, which reads: "You shall not kill."[1]

At first glance, all Jesus seems to do with this commandment is make it stricter and make the punishment for violating it more severe. Quite frankly, His "rewriting" of this commandment does not strike us as "good news":

> You have heard the commandment imposed on your forefathers, "You shall not commit murder; every murderer shall be liable to judgment." What I say to you is: everyone who grows angry with his brother shall be liable to judgment . . . and if he holds him in contempt he risks the fires of Gehenna.
>
> (*Matthew* 5:21-22)

Our spontaneous reaction to this chilling declaration might well be, "If this is the good news, don't tell us the bad news!" We thought things were tough before; Jesus just made them impossible!

If we get beneath our spontaneous emotional reaction, however, and look at what Jesus is really saying, the good news appears. Under the form of a moralizing, even threatening, sermon — which was probably an effort to meet His hearers (and so many of us) "where they were at" — Jesus is leading us to accept a whole new relationship with God and a final clarification of the destiny to which God is leading us. He does this by changing the law, because the law is where teaching meets life. The method Jesus uses here is to give us first some examples of what we are supposed to do — knowing that this is our first question anyway — and then to lead us through our reflection on the implications of this to a realization that our whole relationship with God is now on a different plane.

Jesus doesn't begin by offering us a new set of commandments to replace the old. He just says the law has a new meaning now. The commandment says "You shall not kill." But now, Jesus teaches, you must not be angry with your brother. It doesn't follow. Is the law concerned with what we do or with what we think? What is wrong with nurturing resentment against my brother in my heart so long as I obey the law and don't hurt him?

Right there we have the difference. Jesus has changed the very object of the law. In the Old Testament the laws God gave His people were directed above all toward teaching people to live together like sensible, decent human beings. The law kept the peace. Its immediate function was to make possible a happy human life on earth. And for this reason its accent was above all on preserving peace and harmony within the community of Israel. If people didn't murder, steal, lie, seduce each other's spouses or allow the passions of greed and lust to build up within them, peace could be preserved. And peace made the good life possible on earth.

The law wasn't exclusively concerned with external actions. *Exodus* 20:17 shows this when it teaches, "You shall not covet . . . " *Leviticus* 19:17 is even more clear: the teaching of Jesus is already previewed here in the admonition, "You shall not bear hatred for your brother in your heart. Though you may have to reprove your fellow man, do not incur sin because of him. Take no revenge and cherish no grudge against your fellow countrymen. You shall love your neighbor as yourself. I am the LORD."

Still, interior attitudes of mind and heart were not the real focus of the Jewish law. Covetous desires, anger, resentment, etc. were forbidden, not so much because of what they were in themselves, as because of what they might lead to. Anger might lead one to kill. Lustful thoughts might lead one into adultery. Therefore they were to be avoided.

Jesus changes this. He doesn't just go a step farther, as if He were working within the framework of the existing law and simply raising its tone a bit. What Jesus preaches is not just a more generous way to observe the law, a goal of greater purity of heart to aim at. He doesn't present His teaching as an exhortation to observe the law more perfectly than the law itself requires. He is not proposing something "extra," a higher level for the elite to embrace for themselves. He presents His teaching as being the law itself — the new law of the Kingdom. He emphasizes the distinction between the old law and His own: "You have heard the commandment imposed on your forefathers . . . But what I say to you is . . . " And He repeats this formula again and again. He is making a contrast. He is giving a hint. He is saying, "There is something different about this; look for it."

What is different? It is not the wording of the law. Jesus did not write a new set of commandments. But what He teaches does not follow the commandments that are given. The explanation is that Jesus has changed the whole *basis* of the law, and of its interpretation, by changing its *goal.* The law is no longer based on what is natural and proper for human beings. Its goal is no longer to promote the good life on earth by making it possible for people to live healthy, harmonious lives together in community. The law is now based on what is natural and proper to God Himself, and its goal is personal union with God.

Interior attitudes are the key to it all. The immediate object of the law is no longer peace and harmony within the community, the good life upon earth. The object of the law is *conformity of mind and heart with God.* As soon as the conformity of one's own heart with God's is broken, the law is broken. The reason for avoiding anger, resentment, lust and greed is no longer that these interior attitudes lead to external behavior that disrupts the peace of the community and lowers the quality of life on earth. The reason is that these interior states of soul, if they are personal acts (that is, if they are assented to, embraced with the will and accepted as the expression of what one freely chooses to be) disrupt our harmony with God and break the union of our minds and hearts with His.

To make doubly sure that no one interrupts His teaching as just an exhortation to greater purity of heart, to greater holiness in observing the law, Jesus assigns to His precepts the punishments due to violation of the law. While it was always an ideal in Israel not to carry anger or hatred in one's heart, the law prescribed no punishment for these interior attitudes. It was only when hatred erupted into external violence that the law imposed a sanction. But Jesus teaches that we will be judged and punished, not just on the basis of what we do, but on the basis of what we are in our minds and in our hearts: "What I say to you is: everyone who grows angry with his brother shall be liable to judgment . . . and if he holds him in contempt he risks the fires of Gehenna." Jesus' new teaching *is* the law. He is not just exhorting His hearers to go beyond the law in greater fidelity to the spirit which inspires it. He is giving them a new law. He is not just another rabbi commenting on the law of Moses; He is the new Moses, and in His teaching the law that was given on Mount Sinai is transcended. In the Sermon on the Mount Jesus is a new Moses, giving to the world a New Law.

The goal of Jesus' law is not the good life on earth; it is shared life with God. It is not community among men, but communion with God (which in turn leads to community among men: see *Ephesians* 1:10).

Good behavior is not its focus, nor does violation consist primarily in bad behavior. The focus is simply oneness of heart and soul with God, and any disruption of this union is already a violation of the law at its very core. The law of Jesus is a law of interior conformity to God, and when one no longer chooses to be united with God in mind and heart and will the law is broken. External behavior is just an expression of this. The violation is not in the behavior, or in what one does against others, but in the interior act of breaking off one's union of soul with God.

Implicit in this is the good news about grace. To be one with God in mind and heart, like Him in the thoughts that we think and in the way that we love, this is beyond all human achieving:

> For my thoughts are not your thoughts,
>   nor are your ways my ways, says the
>   LORD.
> As high as the heavens are above the
>   earth,
> so high are my ways above your
>   ways
> and my thoughts above your
>   thoughts.   (*Isaiah* 55:8-9)

The only way we can think or love or act like God is by receiving this favor as a pure gift. And it is the gift of shared life with God. (Compare, for example, *Deuteronomy* 4:5-8 with 1 *Corinthians* 1:17-25 and 4:9-13).

No creature can think and love on the level that is proper to God. God Himself cannot give to any creature the power to do this. God's way of thinking and loving is His very being; it is His life. To think and to love as God does, therefore, is to *be* God. And God Himself cannot create another God.

So the only way God can enable us to think and love as He does, to be truly one in mind and heart with Him, is to come and *join Himself to us.* God must come and "dwell in us," or "abide in us" in such a way that He can think and love within us while catching us up into His own knowing and loving act. We can only think and love like God by sharing in God's own personal acts of knowing and loving as He performs them.

This is what we mean by "grace." It is the favor of sharing in the life of God by being united to the Father, the Son and the Spirit through the gift of their indwelling in our heart. To receive grace is to live on the level of God by sharing in His life as He lives it within us. Or, to say the same thing from a different direction, we become one with the Father, Son and Spirit by being grafted into Christ like branches into the vine, in order to live "in Him," by His life, the way the branches live by the life of the vine or the members of a body live by the life of the whole. The gift of grace is a mystery of oneness with God (see *John* 14:23-26 and 15:1-8).

This explains why Jesus had to change the whole basis and goal of the law. The law that was given through Moses was a law proper for human beings: the law that human beings should live by. But the law given to us by Jesus Christ is the law that is proper to God: the law that God Himself lives by. This is and must be the law of all those who live by grace, because to live by grace is to live as a member of Christ, as His Body on earth. And the Body of Christ must live by the law of Jesus its head, which is the law of the life of God.

Everything Jesus says, then, about the way His disciples should live is an instruction about how to think and act in the way that is proper to God. The basis for this new law is the fact of our union with God; the goal of this new law is to keep us united with God. Union with God in mind and heart and will, in interior attitudes and in the external behavior which expresses them, this is for the disciples of Jesus the beginning and the end of all law.

When Jesus tells us, therefore, that the commandment which used to say, "You shall not kill" is now a commandment which says, "You shall not even be angry with your brother," He has not made the law more severe. He has not taken a law made for human beings and added more weight to its burden. What He is really telling us is that we must live by a new law now because we have been made, by grace, a "new creation" (see 2 *Corinthians* 5:17). We must live by the law of God's life because we have received God's life. That is not bad news but good. It is the good news the world was made for.

Nor is Jesus announcing a more severe punishment for sin. At first glance He seems to be. When He says that anyone who holds his brother in contempt "risks the fires of Gehenna," we take this to refer to the everlasting punishment of hell — which is worse than anything the Sanhedrin could do to a person.[2] We wonder where the "good news" is in this!

The key to understanding this text is to look, not at *how much* one is punished for sin, but at *how*. In the Israel of the Old Testament, sin was punished on this earth, here and now. The punishment was either inflicted by the community (see *Exodus,* chapters 21 and 22 for example) or by God Himself in this life (see for example *Numbers* 20:12; 21:6; and *Deuteronomy,* chapter 28). There was no very clear idea of punishment after death. By the same token, there was no very clear idea of reward after death either. Death itself was the greatest punishment God could inflict on anyone, and a "long life" was the greatest blessing (see *Deuteronomy* 30:20). Among the Jews there was a belief in life after death, but the abode of the dead — *Shoel,* which we translate "Hades" or sometimes "hell" (not meaning here a place of eternal punishment; but rather what the word means when we say in the Creed: "He descended into hell . . . ") — was a shady place, not desirable at all, where the dead were presumed to lead a "diminished existence, without a real relationship with God."[3] The Psalmist reflects very well the tone of the Jewish attitude toward death when he sings, "For among the dead no one remembers you; in the nether world who gives you thanks?" (*Psalms* 6:6; see also *Psalms* 115:17).

When Jesus announced the existence of hell, then (the hell that we ordinarily speak of, the hell of everlasting punishment), He was also announcing the existence of heaven. If sin is punished after death, then it follows that those who accept the good news of the Kingdom will be rewarded after death. Suddenly life takes on a new dimension. Man's existence is no longer bounded by birth and death; our beatitude is no longer limited to the happiness we can enjoy on this earth. Death itself ceases to be the closing-off of all joy and becomes instead an opening-up into the eternal ecstasy of heaven. Now instead of the Psalmist it is St. Paul who gives expression to the attitude God's People take toward death: "O death, where is your victory? O death, where is your sting?" Death, he tells us, is "swallowed up in victory" (1 *Corinthians* 15:54-55).

This is the good news: that each one of us is called to live to God, not just to a human community;

that each one of us answers to God, and not just to society; that the reward of faithful response to God is beatitude forever and ever in heaven, and not just the blessing of a long and happy life on earth; and that God Himself will be our reward, and not just something either God or society can give.

This last idea — that after death God Himself will be our reward, and not just something God can give — is certainly not explicit in the words of Jesus we are reflecting on, and I am not suggesting that anyone just listening to this part of the Sermon on the Mount would have seen it. But from the vantage point of everything else we know, we can look back and see that it is already implicit in this text.

The key is in the contrast. And the contrast is between the whole picture of law and punishment in the Old Testament and in the Gospels. In the Old Testament the object of the law is to promote peace and harmony within the community of Israel. And this is for the sake of the good life here on earth. It follows that if anyone disturbs the peace of the community by sin — that is, by breaking the law — the community must react. Any offense against the law was to be punished here and now, and by the community. That was logical.

In the Gospels the object of the law is union with God. And this union is in reality the union of grace, the favor of sharing in God's own life. Because grace is a share in God's life, grace is the favor of everlasting life. God's life is eternal by nature; to share in it is to live forever, enjoying His own beatitude. That is what we mean by heaven.

In the Gospels, any act which breaks our union of heart and mind with God is a sin, is against the new law. As soon as we are in disharmony with God, even in thought or in desire (provided these are personal acts: free, deliberate choices) we are going against that union of grace which is the purpose of the law and we are guilty of sin. If it is just a matter of slight disharmony with God, our sin does not break our union with God, it just diminishes it. But if in our thoughts and desires we deliberately choose to be something that is simply incompatible with grace, totally contrary to a union of shared life with God, then our union with Him is broken: we are "separated" from God. And this is "deadly" sin: it is sin that "kills" the life of God within us (see 1 *John* 5:14-17).

What we are saying here, if we are alert to it, is that the punishment of sin is already present as soon as the sin is committed. To sin is to distance oneself from God — or to separate oneself from God. The punishment of this sin is inherent in the sin itself; it is to be at a distance from God, or to be separated from God. And this is the whole Christian doctrine of retribution for sin.

To be separated from God in the total, absolute sense of completely losing our union with Him by grace, this is all we mean by "hell." In this life our separation from God cannot be final; we can always repent, and God will keep calling us to repentance. But once we have died, all choices are over. Then, if we are in a state of separation from God, that condition lasts forever. And that is the essential Christian teaching about hell.

This separation from God (like absolute solitary confinement on this earth) is the most painful condition a human being can endure, simply because everything within us was made for God, or for the enjoyment of those creatures whose goodness is an echo of God's voice. Death separates us from all creatures. And if we have also separated ourselves from that union with God which we had by grace, then after death and without God nothing that we are can find satisfaction.

During this life the pain of hell — of separation from God through sin — is not always present to our consciousness, because we can find, not complete satisfaction, but distraction in created imitations of God. The world is an anaesthetic, or can serve as such. And so, by gratifying our physical and psychological appetites through union with creatures on this earth we can find some pleasure and relief. But after death there is no creature that we are in communication with; our satisfaction must come from God Himself or from nothing. "Hell" means simply to exist forever absolutely alone. "Heaven" means to exist forever in the closest possible union with God and with all creatures who also are in union with Him.[4]

By the same line of reasoning, any "distance" from God which we have caused within ourselves by less serious choices in disharmony with His mind and heart is already its own punishment also. To be united with God is our life; to be totally one with Him is our beatitude. Anything which keeps us from total union, total oneness of mind and heart and will with God is a diminishment of our life and of our joy. And this diminishment continues until through the purification of a more complete conversion we are brought into total harmony with God.

This conversion is a conversion to live by absolute faith, hope and love; that is, to live purely by the mind and heart and will of God in the total surrender of ourselves to Him in grace. Until that surrender is complete, we endure the "penalty" consequent upon all sin; namely, a lack of total union with God. Every sin that we repent of is forgiven. But every sin has a tendency to obscure our faith, diminish our hope and weaken our love. These consequences of sin do not just disappear when we are forgiven. They constitute between ourselves and God a barrier which must be overcome. And the process of overcoming that barrier can be painful. It is what we mean by "purification."[5]

We see, then, that in the Sermon on the Mount Jesus is not simply making the law more strict and its punishments more severe. On the contrary, He is announcing — in an implicit way which met His hearers "where they were at" — the good news of the Kingdom. This is the good news of grace, of our call to share in the life of God through union with Him "in Christ." The new law is the law of God's own divine life, and its object is to preserve and promote the union of our minds and hearts and wills with His own. To go against the law is to diminish or destroy our union with God. To keep the law is to be united with Him in the beatitude of His own divine life both now and forever. And this is the good news behind our Lord's revision of "you shall not kill."[6]

FOOTNOTES

[1] Christians number the Commandments differently, according to the tradition of the various denominations. For Catholics this is the Fifth Commandment. In the Protestant tradition it is the Sixth. The reason for the difference is that the Catholics take Exodus 20:1-6 to be one commandment, while the Protestants divide these verses into two; and the Protestants take Exodus 20:17 to be one commandment, while the Catholics divide the verse into two. It makes no practical difference at all. The sequence of commandments which the Sermon on the Mount seems to follow is, with one exception (see page 59 below), the same as that which Jesus follows in Matthew 19:18-19.

[2] Gehenna was literally a valley to the south of Jerusalem where garbage was burned. But the word is also used metaphorically to designate "a place of punishment by fire, the eschatological punishment . . . " See Xavier Leon-Dufour, *Dictionary of the New Testament,* tr. Terrence Prendergast, (Harper and Row, 1980) under "Gehenna."

[3] See Leon-Dufour, *Dictionary Of The New Testament,* under "netherworld."

[4] I am not denying the existence of fire in hell. Scripture scholars and theologians argue over what this "fire" might be, or how the word is used in the Gospels. All I am saying is that, if there is a "fire" of some sort in hell, then, given the pain of absolute aloneness, the fire is a welcome distraction! Anyone who does not see how this can be does not understand what it means to exist forever absolutely alone.

[5] The best explanation of this that I know of — and, incidentally, of the doctrine of "purgatory" which is so misunderstood by Catholics and Protestants alike — is found in St. John of the Cross, *Dark Night of the Soul,* Book II, chapter 10.

[6] Discipleship lives by prayer. A method for praying over the Ten Commandments is appended to this book (see Appendix I, page 190).

CHAPTER THREE: BE HOLY BECAUSE I AM HOLY —
Matthew 5:21-26

Summary:

1. In the Sermon on the Mount Jesus "rewrites" the Ten Commandments, transforming them. The goal of His New Law is not to bring about peaceful, appropriate human behavior on earth, but union of mind and heart and life with God. Therefore His law is broken whenever our interior attitudes and values are not in conformity with God's.

2. The New Law of Jesus is not stricter, but more sublime. It is a law, not for human behavior, but for divine behavior. That is why it is good news. When Jesus tells us we are expected to think and act like God, He is implicitly announcing the good news of our call to share in the life of God by grace.

3. Sin exists from the moment we deliberately break with or distance ourselves from the mind and will of God, refusing to live by His life. The essence of sin is separation from God. This is also the punishment of sin; to be separated from God forever. The opposite side of this coin is that virtue for a Christian is found in union with God by grace, thinking

and acting on a divine level in union with the mind and heart of God. The reward of Christian virtue is a union of shared life and joy with God forever, which we call "heaven" or "eternal life."

4. Heaven is total union with God. Anything which makes us less conformed to the mind and heart of God, less in harmony with His life in our attitudes, values and desires, must be overcome in order for us to enjoy total union with God in heaven. This is what Christian "purification" consists in. It is a process of surrendering to live by absolute faith, hope and love.

5. All of this is implicit in Jesus' rewriting of the commandment, "You shall not kill" (*Matthew* 5:21-26). He teaches that there is sin from the moment our interior attitude toward our brother is not in conformity with God's. Everything else follows from this.

Questions for paryer and discussion:

1. Do I tend to judge my behavior more in terms of external actions or in terms of interior attitudes? In what ways is my interior attitude toward some people not the same as God's?

2. Can I see that in the Sermon on the Mount Jesus is not making the law stricter but putting it on a whole new footing? Can I rejoice in the fact that we are now called to act, not like human beings but like God? Can I explain in my own words how this fact implies the good news of grace? What is grace? How do I experience it or manifest it in my life?

3. Do I think of sin as carrying with it its own punishment, which is distance (or separation) from God? Or do I think that sin leaves me unchanged, but just in danger of being punished later? What effect would it have on my conduct if I were more conscious that every choice to sin, so long as it is unrepented, diminishes my understanding and appreciation of God?

4. In what concrete ways am I working to conform my interior attitudes to those of God? How much do I read and reflect on the words of Scripture in which God's attitudes are revealed in human form? Do I ever look back and review the thoughts and attitudes of the day, comparing them with the mind and heart of Christ? Is there a time when I could conveniently and consistently do this? (In the shower, for example?)

CHAPTER FOUR

THE GOAL OF INTEGRAL RESPONSE
Be One As I Am One

Jesus turned the commandment against killing into a law of conformity with God's own heart (*Matthew* 5:21-26). He does the same with the commandment which forbids sexual misconduct. At the same time He makes this a law of human wholeness and integrity (*Matthew* 5:27-30).

The commandment "You shall not commit adultery" (*Exodus* 20:14) was a commandment designed primarily to keep peace within the community of Israel. If a man had relations with another man's wife, and the husband found out about it, killing was liable to result. This killing was as likely as not to ignite a family feud which would not end until the killing spread farther than anyone could predict. So minute rules were established to determine just which sexual actions were to be considered offenses, and under what circumstances, and how each offense was to be handled by the community (see *Deuteronomy* 22:13-29, for example, and *Leviticus* 20:10 ff.). The emphasis here, as in the rules which interpreted the commandment "You shall not kill" (see *Exodus* 21:12-36), is on forestalling acts of vengeance and violence within the community, therefore keeping peace and making the good life possible on earth.

Jesus changes this. His emphasis is on conformity of mind and heart with God: "You have heard the commandment, 'You shall not commit adultery.' What I say to you is: anyone who looks lustfully at a woman has already committed adultery with her in his thoughts" (*Matthew* 5:27-28). The new law of Christ is a law of interior purity, of interior likeness to God. The law is broken the minute one's mind is no longer conformed to God's mind, the minute one's heart is no longer in harmony with God's.

We are speaking here of deliberate disharmony. To feel spontaneous sexual desire when looking at another is not to "look lustfully." If one encourages the sexual desire, of course, by continuing to look, that is to come into discord with God.

In the next verses, however, this law of sexual purity reveals itself as a law of *personal wholeness:* "If your right eye is your trouble, gouge it out and throw it away! Better to lose part of your body than to have it all cast into Gehenna" (*Matthew* 5:29). Jesus is repeating here His doctrine of punishment after death, the penalty of separation from God as opposed to some sanction imposed by the community. But He introduces a new element: the contrast between wholeness and fragmentation. It is better, He teaches, to lose the integrity of one's body — to lose a hand or an eye, for example — than to lose one's integrity as a person. And right here we get to the heart of sexual sin.

Sexual, sins are fundamentally fragmentation. They are a matter of saying something with the body that one's mind cannot affirm as true or one's will is not committed to. Sex is a language; it is the symbolic language of love, the language that speaks of self-gift. Lovers give their bodies to one another in sexual intercourse as a way of saying they are making the gift of their whole selves. This is what gives sex its value: it is an expression of pledge, of free, personal commitment. Sex is the physical expression of a free person; it is a "word" of enduring love, a word of self-bestowal that is made flesh.

In the measure that the whole person is not included in this "word," sexual expression falls off from authenticity. When sex is just the expression of body and of emotions, while the mind knows that the gift of self is not truly made, and the will holds back from making this gift, sex is an act of fragmentation.

This is why we have made virginity, or the physical intactness of the body, into a symbol of sexual purity. The fact that one is physically a virgin does not mean one is pure; true wholeness of person requires much more than that. But physical intactness is an appropriate symbol to speak to us of the real purity, the real integrity of the human person, which consists in being all together, whole and entire, in everything one does. If by "virginity" we mean the integrity physical virginity really stands for: the unity and integration of all that we are as human beings — our bodies, emotions, intellect and wills — in every action we perform, then this is a virginity which is not lost in marriage. On the contrary, when two people, in the first sexual giving of themselves in marriage, are saying "Yes!" to one another with everything they are — with their bodies, their emotions, their minds and hearts and wills — then this is not a "deflowering," but the flowering of virginity. It is an experience of wholeness achieved, of everything that one is being joined together in one undivided act of expression which is the word of one's own self-bestowal made flesh.[1]

The philosophers tell us that God is one; that He has no parts. In everything God does, He acts with His whole being at once. There is no interior conflict in God, no part of Him that holds itself back in reserve, nothing that is left out when He gives Himself to another in love. And Jesus holds up this same ideal of perfect integrity to us. Not only in our acts of sexual expression, but in everything we do, our goal as sharers in God's life is to be whole and entire, not to be in division with ourselves, not to hold anything back. To keep our humanity perfectly together, not to act with only one part of it at a time, this is the ideal of perfect human wholeness. And to surrender our humanity totally to God, so that in and through every action we are capable of, God is able to express His own life, His own truth and promise and love, this is the ideal of perfect spiritual gift. It is in this giving of our whole being to God that we arrive at total unity, at that complete wholeness of life in nature and in grace which is what Jesus came to give: "I came that they might have life, and have it in its fullness" (see *John* 10:10).

This is the good news implicit in Jesus' teaching on adultery: not that the law is made more strict, but that the ideal held up to His followers is more sublime. It is the ideal of perfect oneness, perfect integration of body, soul and spirit, which makes man most like God. In making this ideal the new law of His Kingdom, Jesus is proclaiming to the world the mystery of humanity made whole by grace.

FOOTNOTE

[1] This is the theme of my book *The Good News About Sex* (St. Anthony Messenger Press, 1979). See especially chapter 23: "Wholeness as an Ideal: The Symbol of the Virgin."

CHAPTER FOUR: THE GOAL OF INTEGRAL RESPONSE
— *Matthew 5:27-30*

Summary:

1. In the Old Testament the commandment, "You shall not commit adultery" was aimed at keeping peace within the community. In Jesus' New Law the aim is conformity of mind and heart with God. Hence even desires that are impure, if they are deliberately excited or encouraged, are a violation of the law. To embrace such desires with our will is to deliberately accept a disunion of our heart with God's.

2. Jesus' sexual teaching is three things: a) it is a law of interior likeness to God (see #1 above); b) it is a law of human wholeness and personal integration; c) it is a law of "enduring love" (see the following chapter). It is a law of wholeness because sexual sins are essentially fragmentation: a way of acting or of saying something with part of our being while other parts are left out or in contradiction. For example, we can "speak" sexually with our bodies or emotions while our wills are silent about commitment and our minds recognize the inauthenticity of what we are doing. This is self-disintegration, fragmentation.

3. By contrast, sexual purity consists in being whole and entire in every sexual action or expression. This is what "virginity" as a symbol stands for: perfect human wholeness in every thought and action, not only in the sexual area, but in every human activity. This "virginity" is not lost in marriage, but is more fully realized the more fully our whole being — body, emotions, intellect, will and spiritual life — enters into our every act and expression. Hence intercourse in marriage should be the flowering, not the loss, of "virginity." It is an act in which our whole being is united in saying, "Yes!"

4. To be perfectly one, whole and entire in everything we do, is to be like God. God has no parts. In every action God acts with His whole being at once. Thus Jesus' new law of sexual purity is a proclamation of the gift of sharing in God's life by grace.

Questions for prayer and discussion:

1. Do I look upon sexual laws as just taboos, as commandments not to do what is evil? Or do I see them as a teaching on how to be one in mind and heart with God? When I sin or am tempted to sin sexually, do I see the sin mostly as a misuse of the body, or as a choice to be unlike God in my thoughts, judgments and values?

2. When would a sexual act be just an expression of the body and of nothing else? When would it be only an expression of body and emotion? How could a sexual act be an expression of one's body, emotions and intellect and at the same time be in contradiction to one's real faith? Can a sexual act outside of marriage be a real expression of commitment? Is every sexual act outside of marriage an act of personal fragmentation? Is it always experienced as such?

3. Does the word "virginity" express to me total wholeness, fullness of human response (physical as well as spiritual), or does it suggest a diminished human expression? Does the real value which we attach to "virginity" consist just in the fact of not having had intercourse, or is it something more total, more positive than this? What real human value does the word "virginity" suggest or symbolize? Is this value lost in marriage or brought to fulfillment? How?

4. In what way does sexual purity — both in and outside of marriage — help us to be like God? (Do I understand passionate intercourse in marriage as an act of sexual purity? Can intercourse be sexually pure without being a passionate, total response of body as well as of soul?)

CHAPTER FIVE

ESPOUSE AS YOU ARE ESPOUSED
The Sharing of "Enduring Love"

Sexual gestures are a language. And when Jesus takes up the commandments which deal with sex — "You shall not commit adultery . . . You shall not covet your neighbor's wife" — the focus of His teaching is on expression of the heart.

For sexual expression to be an authentic human "word" it must come from an undivided heart. Every sexual "word" is meant to be an integral expression of one's person, in which body, soul and spirit are all united in an unfragmented act of total self-bestowal. For sexual gestures to be authentic, they must be the expression of all that we are: flesh, understanding and choice. And the reality they express is love: the committed gift of ourselves to another person.

Sexual intercourse has this in common with the crucifixion of Jesus: that both are passionate, physical, symbolic gestures of pledge. The meaning of Jesus' self-offering on the cross and the meaning of sexual intercourse are the same. Both say, "This is my body, which is given up for you (see *Luke* 22:19;

1 *Corinthians* 11:24). If the gift of the body did not carry with it the gift of the whole person, both intercourse and the crucifixion of Jesus would be stripped of all value.

In the same way, for the gift of the body — whether in intercourse or on the cross — to mean what it is intended to mean, it must be the expression of a love that is irrevocable. The expression of Jesus' love on the cross was literally love unto death. This was the spirit in which Jesus entered into His passion: "He had loved his own in this world, and would show his love for them to the end" (*John* 13:1). The crucifixion is unintelligible except as an expression of "enduring love" — love that will not be overcome, love that nothing can make one take back. And this is the meaning of intercourse in marriage. Sex is a word of "enduring love."[1]

In the Old Testament divorce was permitted. Jesus will say later, when questioned about this, that in the old law God allowed divorce because of His People's "stubbornness" or "hardness of heart" (*Matthew* 19:8). We would probably translate this reason today as "cultural inertia": God allowed divorce in Old Testament times because it was the long-standing practice of His People, and to go against it would have been culturally impossible for them at that time. There is nothing "harder" than the beaten path, and Jesus will use this image later to explain why His words don't even make a dent in the hearts of people who are completely caught up in their culture (see *Matthew* 13:4, 19).

With the coming of Jesus, however, everything changes. Now nothing is impossible for men because through grace they share in the life of God, and "for God all things are possible" (*Matthew* 19:26; see also *Luke* 1:37 and *Matthew* 17:20). Jesus came, not only to give grace to individual hearts, but to establish a graced community, His Church. Within this new culture, this new human and divine environment, what was impossible before now becomes a realistic ideal. From the very beginning of His ministry on earth, Jesus is already beginning to fulfill God's promise: "See, I make all things new!" (*Revelation* 21:5).[2]

In the Sermon on the Mount, therefore, when Jesus goes on to say that divorce is no longer permitted (*Matthew* 5:31-32), He is announcing good news. And the good news is this: now that men are able to share in the life of God, human beings are able, like God, to speak an irrevocable word of self-creation.

In the beginning, God spoke and the world was made. He said, "Let it be," and it was (see *Genesis,* ch. 1). This is a characteristic of God's word: it is efficacious; it produces its effect (see *Isaiah* 55:11; *Hebrews* 4:12 and 11:3). And when God gives His word as a promise, that promise is irrevocable (see *Isaiah* 54:9-10; *Romans* 11:29).

But the word of human beings is not like this. Human beings speak their word and nothing happens. Or we speak it and change it again. We pronounce what we have decided to be and then do not live up to what we have said. It is characteristic of a human word not to be eternal.

What Jesus announces through the abolition of divorce is power given to man to pronounce an irrevocable word of self-creation. When men and women commit themselves to each other forever in a Christian marriage, it is not the power of their own word that they rely upon; it is the power of Jesus' word which He is speaking within them, and which is indistinguishably united with their own. In the marriage vows there is only one single word of commitment — a human and divine word which is equally the word of Jesus and the word of the human being who pronounces it. As each party to the marriage creates himself or herself as a husband or wife, Jesus who lives united to each one through the intimate bond of grace also utters His word. He utters it with, in and through the word of each partner to the marriage. And His word is irrevocable; nothing can ever make Him take it back. In the person of each spouse it is Jesus who says to the other: "This is my body which is given up for you." And by this word the two become one flesh in a way that no human words can make them.

They are also given the power to live for each other with that "enduring love" which is characteristic of God Himself.[3]

When God revealed His "name" — that is, His innermost personality — to Moses (see *Exodus* 33:18 to 34:7), the two words He used to describe Himself in relationship to men were *hesed* and *emet,* which are translated as "kindness" and "fidelity" or simply as "enduring love" (see *Psalms* 57:4; 86:15; 117; *John* 1:14, 17-18). To make and to persevere in a commitment, therefore — to speak and to live a word of "enduring love" — is as close as man can come to being like God. And this is what Jesus proclaims Christian marriage to be.

In the Old Testament the emphasis in marriage was not on fidelity as such. Obviously, fidelity was a most important element of marriage — so much so that God used the image of spousal love in order to explain to His People both the unrelenting passion of His own love for them and the shame of their unfaithfulness to Him (see *Isaiah* 54:5-10 and 62:5; *Jeremiah,* chapters 2-3, *Hosea,* chapters 1-3). But people did not marry precisely for the sake of entering into a covenant of enduring love; they married in order to seek a fuller, happier life together on earth (see *Genesis* 2:18). The goal of marriage was earthly contentment, and the good spouse was the one who made husband or wife content. Evidence of this is the description of the ideal wife in the last chapter of *Proverbs:* the ideal wife is the one who makes her husband happy, and she does this by creating for him a happy home.

Jesus changed this too. I think it is accurate to say that Jesus changed the nature of marriage itself for Christians by changing its goal. In the Old Testament the goal of marriage was mutual contentment and posterity. In the New Testament the goal of marriage is to help one another attain the perfection of love. And since the perfection of love is held up to Christians in the image of the crucified Christ, there is no reason why a crucifying marriage cannot at the same time be a good marriage; that is, one which is fulfilling its purpose.

These may be scandalous words. As a matter of fact, they were scandalous to Jesus' own disciples when He gave His doctrine on divorce to them (see *Matthew* 20:10). Then, as now, they seem to make marriage something it is better to avoid; for who can be sure of finding a partner for life who will be satisfactory? But if the goal of marriage is not satisfaction, but growth to the perfection of love, then marriage is achieving its purpose as long as it is challenging one to love and to love more generously. As long as a marriage is doing this — and one is able to respond to the challenge — there is no reason for divorce.

We are not trying to be over-simplistic here. Situations do arise in which it is better for Christian partners in marriage to separate. Sometimes a marriage can become destructive to love. The challenge of loving can become, in individual cases, too crushing to carry. Or the partners can get themselves into such a stance toward each other that, for the time being at least, nothing either one does can be lifegiving for the other. Or the children can be suffering damage. In such situations Christian tradition allows separation. But separation is not the same as divorce.

In a separation the partners take a distance from one another. It may turn out that this distance lasts until death, that they never come back together again. But divorce is more than a distancing; it is complete rupture of the bond. It is this that the Gospel forbids.[4]

What Jesus is really saying here is that the love which a man and a woman give to one another in marriage is the exact image of the love which God Himself gives to us who are His People, His Bride, His Body on earth. All throughout the history of Israel God keeps proving to His People that no matter what they do and no matter how much or how terribly they reject Him, He will always take them back, He will always forgive. Never will He renounce the Covenant He made with them. Israel is the Bride of Yahweh, His spouse, and He will never abandon her. He may separate from her for a time — because she has deserted Him and given herself to adulterous lovers (see *Ezekiel,* chapter 16), but He will never renounce her or break off His relationship with her (see *Ezekiel* 16:60). St. Paul continues this imagery when he compares a man's love for his wife with Jesus' love for the Church (see *Ephesians* 5:22-33).[5]

The only thing that can definitely rupture the marriage bond between two spouses is remarriage. As long as neither has remarried, the door to return is still open. It is remarriage which closes the door. That is why it is not separation, but divorce — divorce with the option of remarriage — that the Gospel forbids. Until God breaks off His Covenant with His People and closes the door to their return, Christian spouses are pledged to maintain their bond of commitment to one another and keep themselves open for the other's return. In other words, a Christian marriage is a pledge to love as God loves. It is a visible and lifelong fulfillment of the new commandment of Jesus: "Love one another as I have loved you" (see *John* 13:34 and 15:12).

With this teaching Jesus transcends the commandment: "You shall not covet your neighbor's wife" (*Exodus* 20:17). If no second marriage is possible, even after a separation from one's spouse, then it is useless to dream of how fulfilling life might be with another. But the prohibition of divorce would not be good news at all without the positive element of Christ's teaching which we have explained above: first, the power given to man to speak a "word" of self-creation and of commitment as irrevocable as God's; secondly, the orientation of marriage itself toward growth in love instead of simply toward a good, mutually satisfying life on earth; and above all, the mystery of love that can reach fulfillment even through crucifixion. The mystery of married love is the mystery of God's own love, and its pattern is revealed in the fidelity of Jesus to His People on the cross.

To love as Jesus loves, this is to love like God. To commit oneself to loving like this is to base one's life on the gift of grace. It is to stake one's whole future on the belief that one actually has been united with God in such a way that one is able to love as God loves — to share in God's own life and act of existence as "enduring love." It is to take Jesus seriously in trust when He says, "You must be made perfect as your heavenly Father is perfect" (*Matthew* 5:48). Nothing else, no other hope based on human generosity or fidelity, makes the absolute commitment of Christian marriage acceptable.

This, then, is the good news: not that the law of marriage has become more strict or its commitment riskier. The good news is that God has caught us up into His own life and made us able to utter a word of "enduring love" that is as irrevocable as His own. Christian marriage is a proclamation of our call to live and to love like God.

FOOTNOTES

[1] For a development of this explanation of sexuality, see my book *The Good News About Sex,* especially chapters 13-15 (St. Anthony Messenger Press, 1979).

[2] For the importance of the Church as a saving environment, a milieu of life in which the light and love of God can grow, see my earlier book: *Why Jesus?* chapter 3: "Jesus is Deliverance From Sin" (Dimension Books, 1981).

[3] This theme is dear to my heart. It seems, like the explanation of grace, to enter sooner or later into every book I write. See for example *Lift Up Your Eyes To The Mountain,* pp. 12-13.

[4] This does not mean Christians are forbidden to get a civil divorce. For a separation to be effective, civil divorce may be necessary. But Christians understand marriage to be more than a personal and civic contract. Just as God's uniting word is required to make a Christian marriage authentic, and certification by the state is not enough, so the dissolving of a marriage as a civic contract through judicial divorce is not enough to dissolve the bond Christians enter into. For this reason Christians, even after receiving a civil divorce, still consider themselves to be bound to one another through the "word" they spoke to each other in

union with Christ, and through the word that Christ abiding in each one spoke to the other. This bond cannot be dissolved unless Christ Himself dissolves it: "Therefore, let no man separate what God has joined" (*Matthew* 19:6).

⁵ In Matthew's Gospel Jesus seems to allow divorce under one condition; it is forbidden, He says, "except in the case of *porneia.*" The Revised Standard Version of the Bible translates this: "except on the ground of unchastity." The New American Bible simply says, "Lewd conduct is a separate case." No one can say from the text alone just what the exact meaning of these words is. The word *porneia* in Greek can mean immorality, fornication, or even incest (see 1 *Corinthians* 5:1). I accept the position of those scholars who understand this in the light of Acts 15:20, and interpret it as meaning that those converts from paganism who had married people more closely related to them than the Jewish law allowed could dissolve their union on the grounds that these marriages were invalid anyway; that is, that they were incestuous — hence *"porneia."* One thing is clear from God's dealings with His own spouse, Israel: God does not reject His bride because of infidelity. The prophets are filled with this theme. Neither, then, should we.

CHAPTER FIVE: ESPOUSE AS YOU ARE ESPOUSED — *Matthew* 5:31-32

Summary:

1. By abolishing divorce, Jesus proclaimed man's ability, by grace, to speak a word of "enduring love" — that is, to speak a word of commitment, of self-creation, as efficacious and as irrevocable as God's own word. This was an implicit announcement of the gift of sharing in God's own life by grace.
2. In the Old Testament divorce was allowed because of people's "hardness of heart." With the coming of Jesus, however, two things made it possible for us to commit ourselves in covenants of love as enduring as God's own covenant with His People. First, by the gift of grace we become one with Christ in such a way that when we commit ourselves to another in marriage, Jesus Himself speaks the word of commitment with and in us, as identified with us. Thus our word of commitment carries the power of Jesus' own "enduring love." We love and commit ourselves "in Him." He loves and commits Himself in us. It is not just we who love, but Christ loves in us. Secondly, in the Church a new community, a new milieu, a new cultural environment

is established to support us in living out our commitment to "enduring love."

3. The goal of marriage in Old Testament times was a happy, contented life on earth through mutual love and assistance. If the marriage failed to provide contentment, divorce was permitted. By abolishing divorce, Jesus changed the goal and nature of marriage. Marriage is now a school of "enduring love," and its goal is to help both parties become able to love as God does, perfectly. This love is compatible with crucifixion, as Jesus showed us.

4. Christian marriage is an image of Christ's love for His Church. God never rejects His People or Christ His Church because of sin. Neither should married couples reject each other because of sin. Christian marriage is a commitment to live out visibly for life Jesus' commandment to "love one another as I have loved you." As such it is impossible without grace, and is a visible witness to belief in the presence and power of grace. Married couples base their whole lives on the mystery of grace at work within them.

Questions for prayer and discussion:

1. Do I believe it is possible for human beings to commit themselves irrevocably to one another in love? Would such a commitment have to rest on trust in a power of loving — of healing and of unifying — that is more than human? Does making such a commitment bear witness to belief in the presence and power of grace? Does it show an understanding of what the "grace of Jesus Christ" is all about? (see *Ephesians* 1:9-10 and 2:11-22).

2. How does our union with Christ in grace make it possible for us to commit ourselves irrevocably in love? How can the Christian community help people to live by this commitment?

3. How does the goal of marriage for Christians differ from that which appears in the Old Testament? (Compare *Proverbs* 31:10-31 with *Ephesians* 5:22-33). If we understand marriage to be a school of love, how does this affect our understanding of divorce? In what image did Jesus show us the perfection of love? How would this apply to marriage? What characteristics do the crucifixion of Jesus and sexual intercourse have in common?

4. Did God reject Israel in favor of a new Bride, the Church? Or is the Church just the fulfillment of God's promises to Israel, and the New Covenant the transformed continuation of the Covenant with Israel, open to all? (See Romans, chapters 9-11). If no sin will make God reject His people, His Bride, can any sin justify the rejection of one spouse by another in a Christian marriage?

CHAPTER SIX

BE SIMPLE BECAUSE YOU ARE SACRED
This Is My Word, Spoken From Your Heart

When Jesus abolished divorce He proclaimed, in effect, that through union with God in grace man is now able to speak eternally enduring "words" of commitment and of love. A word of commitment is a word of self-determination which endures. To commit oneself, therefore, is to create oneself. To commit oneself forever is to speak a word of self-creation which endures forever. Like God, we say, "Let it be" and it is: "Let us be this," and we are.

There is something about us, however, which does not attach much value to our words — or to the words of others. We feel that a human word as such is not very convincing; that a word of promise unsupported by anything else does not inspire trust. We seem to take the position, consciously or not, that neither our words nor our persons are all that sacred in themselves.

That is perhaps why Jesus breaks the sequence of the commandments here. Instead of going on to the next commandment in Exodus: "You shall not steal,"

He chooses rather to follow up His teaching on commitment — His declaration of the value and force of man's personal word — with a transformation of the commandments that deal with speech.

There are two of these: "You shall not take the name of the LORD, your God, in vain," and "You shall not bear false witness against your neighbor" (*Exodus* 20:7, 16). Leviticus combines these into one: "You shall not lie or speak falsely to one another. You shall not swear falsely by my name . . . " (*Leviticus* 19:11-12). The teaching of Jesus is that we should not swear at all: "Say 'Yes' when you mean 'Yes' and 'No' when you mean 'No.' Anything beyond that is from the evil one" (see *Matthew* 5:33-37).

We back up our statements with oaths because we don't think our own words — or our own persons — are sacred enough. We swear by someone higher than ourselves, or by something we hold to be more sacred than just our given word. We swear by heaven because it is God's throne; by the earth because it is His footstool; by our own heads, as if there were more power in them than in the rest of us. And the Old Testament commandments seem to support us in this tendency: all they say is that we must not give false testimony against our neighbor, and that, if we do swear to anything by God's name, we must fulfill what we promise and not use His name to swear to anything untrue (*Exodus* 20:7 and 16; *Numbers* 30:3).

The emphasis of these commandments is on telling the truth and keeping intact the bond of trust-worthiness that society is built on. No one's dignity is in direct focus except God's: "You shall not swear falsely by my name, thus profaning the name of your God. I am the LORD" (*Leviticus* 19:12). Jesus changes these commandments.

First of all, His emphasis is not on the need for truthfulness among men. Certainly society cannot exist unless people can be relied upon. Law courts in particular could not function if there were not some basic assurance that witnesses will tell the truth. But the new commandment of Jesus goes beyond all this. He focuses, not on the need for truthfulness in society, but on the need we seem to have to back up the dignity of our word by appealing to the dignity of something or of someone else outside of us.

Jesus tells us to renounce this need. "What I tell you is: do not swear at all . . . Say, 'Yes' when you mean 'Yes' and 'No' when you mean 'No.' Anything beyond that is from the evil one" (*Matthew* 5:34-37).

In doing this, His purpose is not to protect the dignity of God; it is to proclaim the dignity of man become one with God by grace. This new commandment is focused on the sacredness of human words. But by giving a new teaching about the value of our words, Jesus is giving a new teaching about our own value as persons in grace.

We are the Body of Christ, the temple of the Holy Spirit, the true children of the Father. We have the dignity of Christ Himself, because we have been made one with Him the way the various parts of the body are one with the head. We need not, and we should not, swear by anything outside of ourselves, because we are one with Christ. Our words have the sacredness that belongs to His person, and to swear by anything else is implicitly to deny what we are.

"Men swear by someone greater than themselves," the letter to the Hebrews argues. And so, "when God made his promise to Abraham, he swore by himself, having no one greater to swear by" (*Hebrews* 6:13-16). If we, then, are the Body of Christ, there is nothing on earth that has any greater sacredness that is essentially different from our own. Ours is the sacred dignity of the Body of Christ. Our words draw their sacredness from that. If we swear by anything outside of ourselves we appear to be saying that our words do not have the sacredness that actually belongs to them as expressions of the Body of Christ. This makes every oath an act of forgetting who we are.

There is in Christ's teaching here a combination of reverence and humility. On the one hand, we should have so much respect for God, and for the sacredness that all creation has through its relationship to God, that we would not swear by anything at all. To swear by heaven is the same as swearing by God, for heaven is God's throne. And earth is just as sacred as heaven, for it is God's footstool. Nothing exists that is not what it is because of its relationship to God. We should not swear lightly by anything at all, therefore. This reverence is an act of humility before the sacredness of all that is.

On the other hand, if we value our own sacredness as we should — which also is reverence, and not pride — we should realize that nothing on earth is more sacred than the simple human word, because nothing on earth shares more in the reality and life of God than people do. By nature we are in the image of God: free, choosing, rational creatures. Our "words" of decision and choice are truly acts of self-creation, utterances with a power like that of the words of God. By grace we are the Body of Christ, sharers in God's own life; and this makes our words acts of co-utterance with God. For us who are graced children of God and members of Christ, therefore, to swear by anything at all would seem to be an implicit denial of the sacredness of our words, a forgetful ignoring of our human and graced reality.

What Jesus is preaching here is not the attitude of those whose word is their bond simply because they are proud. Unless we are deeply rooted in a sense of our own creatureliness, of our dependence on God for every breath we take in and every word we breathe out, as well as for every action we have strength to perform, there can be arrogance behind the insistence that our words are as irrevocable as God's. Herod fell into this trap when he swore to a dancing girl that he would give her anything she asked, even to half of his kingdom. It made him a murderer (see *Mark* 6:23).

When we insist on the value of our simple word, it is not because we have an exaggerated sense of our personal sovereignty, a pride of personalism so strong that we pretend there is nothing which could deflect us from our course. Jesus reminds us of this, and of the essential dependency of our condition as creatures, when He says, "Do not swear by your head, for you cannot make a single hair white or black" (see *Matthew* 5:36).

Some Christians take the teaching of Jesus here to be a rule, and they observe it literally, refusing to ever take any oath at all. But Jesus is not making rules in the Sermon on the Mount. What He is really doing is proclaiming the good news of who we are, of what we have become by grace. He does this by drawing some practical conclusions from the commandments that exist, but in such a way that His conclusions don't logically follow from the law unless we see the law itself as having a whole new basis and goal. He doesn't replace the Ten Commandments with a new set of rules. He transforms our understanding of the Commandments by replacing the concept we have of ourselves. Once we know ourselves as united to God by grace and called to live and act on the level of God Himself, we bring an entirely new approach to our interpretation of the Ten Commandments. They are no longer norms for good human behavior, but starting points for a reflection on the behavior that is proper to God. Their aim is no longer the good life on earth in a society characterized by peace. Their goal is union of mind and heart and will with God.

From this point of view, the important question is not whether we should ever swear an oath at all, for any reason, but rather how we are to understand the value of our words and the sacredness of our persons. The conversion asked of us in this passage of the Sermon on the Mount is not a conversion in the area of speech only, but above all in the area of our self-understanding. If we can see ourselves as Jesus sees us, and remain conscious always of the sacredness that is ours through union with Him, then not only our language, but our every act of self-expression will be transformed.

This is discipleship: not to conform mechanically to rules, but to change in understanding and appreciation. Our efforts as disciples should be, not just to obey, but to grow in likeness to the mind and heart of Christ. It is from this interior likeness to Him that all our behavior should flow.

CHAPTER SIX: BE SIMPLE BECAUSE YOU ARE SACRED
— *Matthew* 5:33-37

Summary:

1. The Old Testament commandments "You shall not take the name of the LORD, your God, in vain," and "You shall not bear false witness against your neighbor" have as their focus two things: respect for God and for the practical need for

truthfulness between people if they are going to live together in society. In His new teaching about speech, Jesus puts the focus on the sacredness of man himself and of every human word.

2. Our tendency is to attach very little value to an unsupported human word, even our own. We feel we have to swear by something more sacred than ourselves in order for our words to become sacred. Since we believe, however, that grace has made us the Body of Christ and temples of the Holy Spirit, any act of swearing by something outside of ourselves appears as a forgetfulness, if not an implicit denial, of what we are. To let our words stand on their own value as a simple "yes" or "no" is a way of professing the sacredness of our persons in union with Christ.

3. Jesus' teaching here is not a rule, a simple prohibition against saying anything stronger than "yes" or "no." It is a proclamation of our union with God by grace. Not only our words, but our every act of self-expression should be worthy of the Body of Christ which we are.

4. Because we are the Body of Christ, every graced word we speak is an act of co-utterance with Christ, and carries with it the sacredness of Christ's own words. It is not we alone who speak, but Christ speaks in us; just as in all our graced behavior it is not we alone who act or live but Christ who lives and acts in us. Christ's teaching here is a reminder of this.

Questions for prayer and discussion:

1. What value do I attach to my words? Am I conscious that when I speak Christ is speaking in and with me? What does it mean to say this? What does it not mean?

2. Which contributes more to growth in understanding Christ and the spiritual life: to see Jesus' teaching here as a simple rule forbidding oaths of any kind, and to obey it as such; or to see it as a way of saying something about the sacredness of life in grace and to ponder on its implications? Which makes more demands on us? Why?

3. Does any way of speaking that I engage in tend to make me less conscious of my own sacredness as the Body of Christ? Does impatience with others do this? Bad language? How can appealing to some other sacred reality to give value to my words have this effect?

4. What practical decisions can I make about my way of speaking that will help me grow in awareness of my sacredness as the Body of Christ, called to act in union with Jesus in everything I do? Do I choose to make these decisions? Why?

CHAPTER SEVEN

PERFECT LOVE CASTS OUT JUSTICE
After God, Relationship With Others

Most wars are fought over money, but those who engage in them usually see themselves fighting for something else — like justice or freedom. As a member of the Texas militia wrote home to his family at the outbreak of that state's war for independence from Mexico: "If we win we will all be rich; if we lose, we will have died for freedom!"

Both sides of this revealing statement could be true. It is possible to go to war for the freedom to make more money, or even for the freedom to retain what is rightfully one's own. But when the oppressed and exploited masses of this world turn to revolt, the cry on their lips is "Justice!" They may be starving and homeless; they may see their children deprived of all chance for improvement. But what finally ignites their spirits into flame and sends them out to the barricades to risk their lives in conflict is a sense of outrage at injustice. If they win, they hope for a better material standard of living; but if they lose, their consolation is they died for justice.

The new law of Jesus takes us beyond justice. Jesus uses the commandments which deal with property to revise our whole thinking with regard to property rights, the defense of all rights, and the place of justice in our lives.

When Jesus takes up the commandments "You shall not steal . . . You shall not covet your neighbor's house . . . nor anything else that belongs to him" (see *Matthew* 5:38-42 and *Exodus* 20:15, 17) His focus is not on property at all. It is on the tension between justice and relationship. And this tension is a fact of everyday experience.

Property is certainly one, at least, of the most frequent sources of disputes among people. Brothers and sisters stop talking to each other because of arguments over inheritance. Good friends go into business together and soon they are not friends any more. Neighbors stop being good neighbors when the pets of one family become a threat to the garden of another. If people never fell out with each other over money, property damage or disputed ownership, half of the divisions in the world would disappear.

The aim of Old Testament law was to prevent violence from erupting out of injustice. The aim of Jesus' law is to bypass the question of justice entirely and focus on relationship instead. Relationship with others should be more important to us than squaring accounts after an injury or insult: "When a person strikes you on the right cheek, turn and offer him the other." We should accept the loss of any material thing rather than break off our relationship with another person: "If anyone wants to go to law over your shirt, hand him your coat as well." And relationship with people should be more important to us than every infringement on our time: "Should anyone press you into service for one mile, go with him two miles" (see *Matthew* 5:38-42). Teaching like this is not just news; it is a revolution in attitudes and values. And it came as such to those who listened to Jesus.

From the beginning of human history "Justice!" has been a spontaneous war-cry of the human heart.

Nothing will provoke a person to violence faster than the conviction that he has been made the victim of injustice. For this reason peace in any community depends on a set of very careful provisions for righting wrongs and restoring the balance when someone has suffered loss at the hands of another.

This concern for maintaining peace in the community is very obvious in the laws of Israel. When it was foreseen that a particular kind of injury was liable to provoke a violent revenge, the law provided for punishment violent enough to satisfy the offended party, but not so violent that the offender would have reason to feel that he, in his turn, had suffered an injustice. The punishments of the law were a counterfire to keep the fire of violence from spreading (see *Exodus,* chapter 21, for examples).

It is in the nature of violence to multiply. Chapter four of Genesis makes this pretty clear.[1] If one man kills another, the victim's relatives will avenge the murder, not with one death, but with seven. Cain's son, Lamech, boasts that he himself will be avenged, not seven times, but "seventy times seven." In this context, the law's provision of "an eye for an eye, a tooth for a tooth" (see *Leviticus* 24:17-22) appears restrained. And indeed it was. Harsh as it may sound to us, it was a very wise and pragmatic provision for keeping retaliation within bonds.

Jesus refers to the old law with its concern for justice through exact retribution, and then He goes beyond it. "You have heard the commandment, 'An eye for an eye, a tooth for a tooth.' But what I say to you is: offer no resistance to injury. When a person strikes you on the right cheek, turn and offer him the other. If anyone wants to go to law over your shirt, hand him your coat as well. Should anyone press you into service for one mile, go with him two miles. Give to the man who begs from you. Do not turn your back on the borrower" (*Matthew* 5:38-42).

This is a radical new teaching. It is radical because it addresses the root of our relationship with each other. It makes relationship with others in love, and not fair dealing in justice, the basis of human society. What Jesus is giving here is not just a new law, or a new rule of conduct; it is a new principle, a whole new basis on which to establish all our rules of conduct. He is teaching us a new stance of mind and heart and will toward one another.

If anyone needs convincing that the Sermon on the Mount was never intended to be a new set of rules, this passage should do it. The early Christian communities did have rules. St. Paul himself made some for the various churches he established, suited to the customs of the time and place (see 1 *Corinthians,* chapters 6-14, for example). But there is no evidence that the Christians ever considered it a specific rule of their religion to literally turn the other cheek when slapped, or never to dispute with another in court over property rights. (When St. Paul reproves the Christians of Corinth for taking each other to court, it is because they were making pagans, not other Christians, their judges. But he does exhort them in the spirit of the Sermon on the Mount to let themselves be cheated and to put up with injustice rather than fall out with one another. See 1 *Corinthians* 6:1-11).

What Jesus is giving here is not a new set of rules, but a number of examples to illustrate and lead us to a general principle. Jesus gives us the examples; we have to discover the general principle for ourselves. In this way He leads us into discipleship; He encourages us to think.[2]

If we think about the examples in this passage, we realize that Jesus is giving us a whole new attitude toward justice. Justice in the Ten Commandments was condensed into the law: "You shall not steal" *(Exodus* 20:15). It was then expanded into many laws designed to help settle disputes arising over personal injury, property damage, theft, loans and even sexual seduction (see *Exodus* 21-22). The aim of all these legal provisions was a justice that would preserve the peace. For that reason, and because all of Israel's laws were the laws of a God whose purpose was to lead people closer to Himself, the justice of the law was always tempered with compassion.

The teaching of Jesus throws our thinking onto another plane entirely. It is revolutionary. What Jesus tells us is to forget about justice entirely and think only of relationship with our fellow man.

His principle is this: nothing on this earth should be more important to us than maintaining our relationship with other people. We should not allow this relationship to be broken off or strained by any dispute over property. No material thing (even the shirt on our back!) should be more important to us than the love of our brother or sister. We should not allow our relationship with another to be called into question by any demands made on our time: if someone infringes on our precious time by making us go one mile out of our way, we should go another mile, just to show that our brother or our sister is more important to us than our time. And (hardest of all) we should not withdraw from a relationship because of any personal insult or injury. If we offer our friendship to another and it is rejected in a way that is as insulting as a slap in the face, we should offer it again. And again, and again, and again. Our sense of pride, of rejection or of offended honor should not be more important to us than achieving a strong relationship of love with every human being we know.

This ideal of love is not difficult for us; it is impossible! It is impossible because it is the love that God Himself lives by. No material thing on earth is worth more to God than the relationship He desires to have with each one of us. And God created time for one purpose only: to bring people into relationship with Himself. We are more important to Him than all the wealth and hours in the world.

God will not even reject us for insulting Him. The response God makes to blasphemy, indifference, scepticism, insult or rejection of His grace is to offer Himself again. We see this in the life of Jesus. Up to the last breath that He drew on the cross He was offering Himself for those who rejected Him. And the Scripture tells us He is interceding for us still (see *Hebrews* 7:24-25; 1 *John* 2:1-2). What Jesus is presenting to us here is not a new law of justice, but a law of love which takes no account of justice. This is the law of God's own heart.

This law is impossible for us, yet not impossible. As we have seen Jesus saying in another context, "For man it is impossible; but for God all things are possible" (*Matthew* 19:26). We act now with the power of God because of our union with Him by grace.

If Jesus were giving rules here, we would have to make a judgment about whether they can realistically be put into practice. Is it realistic to say that a person should *never* go to court with someone who wants to take the shirt off his back? Or never stop coming back for more, no matter how many times one is rejected? Can we put no limits at all on how often we will allow another person to take up our time? Don't we have to measure these declarations of Jesus against our obligations to other people, the fulfillment of our own needs, etc.?

If these were rules, we would simply have to live up to them as they are written, to the best of our ability. Even rules, of course, are to be obeyed with common sense. But when a law is worded in such a way that it obviously intends to call for radical conduct, we should presume that the lawmaker wants us to carry out his rule against all other considerations. If the marines get a command, "Hold your position to the death," the presumption is that they are supposed to do just that. And the less they think about it, the better.

If Jesus had meant these statements to be rules, they would have become the standard practice of all Christians, and Christians would be identified as people whose custom it is to do these particular things. Or the community of believers would have silently judged these commands to be unrealistic and simply ignored them as ideals too high to think about putting into practice. Rules are like that: you either keep them or you don't. If you don't — or can't — do what the rule says to do, you just ignore it.

But principles are different. A principle doesn't legislate what you are to do; it tells you how to approach a problem. A principle establishes priorities;

it tells you what your attitudes and values should be. From a clear set of principles, one is able to work toward a practical decision.

I once asked a young seminarian who had served time in prison before his conversion whether "turning the other cheek" was the way to maintain good relationships with people in prison. "No way," he told me: "They talk another language there."

It could be that the fastest way to rupture your relationship entirely with a friend or business associate would be to let him cheat you. If you know he is wrong, and he knows he is wrong, and neither of you says anything about it, the chances are you will not be friends or partners very long.

But if these words of Jesus are taken for what they are: examples of a general principle, then they become, not only realistic, but practical and radical at the same time. They impose no simplistic (and therefore unlivable) particular rules of conduct; what they do is give us a principle to be believed in, embraced, and carried out into action in whatever manner and degree circumstances allow. And this leads to radical behavior. If only a tiny minority of people really lived by this one principle of Jesus, it would revolutionize the world!

The principle says that we should not value anything on earth more than good relationships with our fellow human beings. And therefore we should not enter into any dispute over property or money which would have the effect of diminishing our relationship with another person. (How many families don't talk to each other any more because of some silly argument over an inheritance? How many countries have gone to war, or are ready to go to war, over a bit of land? Or to preserve some asset — such as oil — which they consider "vital to their national interest"?).

There may be a dozen occasions every day when a person has to argue with another over property (professional horsetraders, for example — who are found in many employments!). And very frequently the greater good of one's obligations to other people (or to oneself) may require one to insist on justice even if it means the break-up of a relationship. This is not to put money ahead of people. But there are countless other occasions when we are able to "let the shirt go" — and the coat as well — because we know that it really is an act of love. When we do that, then not only will we not shame our neighbor by making him look bad, but we ourselves will not be left with resentment in our hearts. The principle is not that we should always give in to another's demands. The principle is that we should give in whenever it will truly foster a relationship — and truly be an act of love.

To accept the principle Jesus teaches here — and not just the concrete actions He proposes as examples — means that we will never just write off His teaching as "unrealistic." Principles are always realistic, because they always presume that we will be pragmatic in our application of them. At the same time, a principle can lead us to most radical, heroic decisions. Especially is this true of the principles Jesus proposes in the Gospels.

That is why discipleship is concerned with principles rather than with rules. Rules are very limited things. It is principles which expand our hearts and minds. Rules are closed in on themselves and tend to close us in as well, while principles are always open-ended. Rules mark the end of a discussion: when a law is passed, Congress adjourns. But principles are always a starting point. Principles lead us into the unknown, pointing us toward undiscovered horizons. We don't know where a principle may lead us. That is why Jesus seldom, if ever, says anything in the Gospels which can be made into a rule (see, for example, *Matthew* 6:19; 8:22; 10:9-10; 19:21; *Luke* 14:26). Jesus deals in principles, because from principles He can lead us into growth, and growth is what discipleship is all about.

In response to the commandments which deal with justice, Jesus offers us a principle which focuses on love. When we focus on love instead of on justice in all our dealings with one another, we have begun to be His disciples (see *John* 13:35), and we are learning to live like God.

FOOTNOTES

[1] For a development of this, see my previous book, *First Steps In Christian Discipleship — The Experience of Accepting Jesus,* chapter ten: "Accepting the Prince of Peace" (Dimension Books, 1982).

[2] I have used this passage from Matthew to teach the "prayer of discipleship," or reflection on the Scriptures, in *His Way,* chapter four: "A Practical Method for Praying Over The Scriptures" (St. Anthony Messenger Press, 1977).

CHAPTER SEVEN: PERFECT LOVE CASTS OUT JUSTICE
— *Matthew* 5:38-42

Summary:

1. The aim of the Old Testament commandments: "You shall not steal" and "You shall not covet your neighbor's goods" was to keep violence from erupting in the community over the question of property. The aim of Jesus' teaching on this commandment is that we should value people, and relationship with people, over all material goods. He teaches us to

focus on relationship with people rather than on justice, and to seek communion with one another in love rather than the defense of our rights.

2. This teaching calls for a radical overturning of our attitudes and values. By history and culture we are conditioned to defend our possessions with violence, to retaliate against injustices. Jesus calls on us to act, not in the way that is natural to human beings, but in the way that is proper to God. As such, His teaching is a proclamation of grace.

3. Jesus' instructions about turning the other cheek, letting go the coat as well, etc. are not rules. They are examples meant to illustrate a general principle. This is His way of teaching throughout the Gospels. To really be disciples, we must try to discover the general principles, the attitudes and values, the mind and heart of Christ behind the concrete things He tells people to do. Rules mark the end of a discussion; principles are a starting point. For discipleship to be a way of growth, it must focus on principles rather than on rules.

4. The general principle Jesus teaches here is that we should not let anything on earth be more important to us than relationship with our fellow man. For example, we should not break off or allow any diminishment in our relationship with others because of disputes over possessions, infringements on our time, or acts of insult or rejection. This ideal is manifestly impossible for human beings. To even strive for it is a witness to our belief that by grace we share in the life and loving power of God.

Questions for prayer and discussion:

1. What concrete issues cause people to break off their relationship with each other? Have I known people to stop talking because of disputes over money or property? Because one person got slapped in the face too often and would not take a chance on being hurt again? Because one didn't have time to spend on the other? How would the teaching of Jesus apply to these situations?

2. Am I able to recognize in my own life — in my past history and present patterns of reaction — an inclination to retaliate against injustice with violence? Are abstract issues, causes, etc. more important to me than concrete people? Do I take sides and treat one group of people as enemies in order to defend the rights of another? Did Jesus ever show Himself inclined to destroy sinners in order to rid the world of sin? How can I imitate Him in this?

3. Do I think Jesus' teaching here is realistic? Is it possible to put relationship with people ahead of all other values (except God)? Would it be realistic to think in terms of beginning with less important issues? Where, concretely, in my life can I begin to put relationship with others ahead of my possessions, my dignity, my time?

4. When I read or hear the Gospels, am I usually in the back of my mind listening for concrete instructions, rules that tell me what to do? Or am I searching for the attitudes and values that inspire the things Jesus teaches? Am I trying to penetrate through the concrete, particular examples to get in touch with the mind and heart of Christ? How could I begin to do this, or begin to do it more deeply?

CHAPTER EIGHT

HONOR YOUR FATHER, YOUR FOE
Love in the Family of God

In chapter nineteen of Matthew's Gospel a young man asks Jesus which commandments he must keep to have eternal life. It is curious to note that in His response Jesus lists the commandments in the same sequence which He appears to follow in the Sermon on the Mount. He begins in the middle of the Old Testament list (see *Exodus* 20:1-17) with the commandment "You shall not kill." Then He goes on to mention adultery, stealing and lying. A glance back through chapters three to seven of this book will show that in the Sermon on the Mount Matthew presents Jesus as following the same order. The exception is that in the Sermon on the Mount the commandments dealing with speech precede the commandment against stealing. We have discussed a possible reason for this (see above, page 60).

A curious thing about the list Jesus recites to the young man in chapter nineteen is that the commandment which concludes the list — "Honor your father and mother" — is found in the original listing of

Exodus before all the ones we have mentioned. Why did Jesus put it last instead of first? And why did He add behind this commandment another one which is not in the Exodus list at all — not one of the Ten Commandments, that is — namely, "Love your neighbor as yourself" (see *Matthew* 19:16-19; *Leviticus* 19:18)?

It would appear that Matthew's intention here is to show Jesus summing up at the end of His list all the commandments which govern our relationship with other people in this world (see *Romans* 13:8-10). The first commandments of the Decalogue are directly focused on our relationship with God: "I, the LORD, am your God . . . You shall not have other gods besides me . . . You shall not take the name of the LORD, your God, in vain . . . Remember to keep holy the sabbath day" (see *Exodus* 20:2-8). The rest of the commandments, beginning with "Honor your father and your mother . . . " concern our relationship with other people. Jesus, however, makes these end, rather than begin, with "Honor your father and your mother . . . " And He adds to the list, as if it belonged there, the *Leviticus* teaching, "Love your neighbor as yourself."

If Jesus' intention was to sum up in one statement all the commandments which teach us how to relate to our neighbor, the change would be logical. "Honor your father and your mother" is the law of *pietas*. This word doesn't mean at all what "piety" suggests to us. What *pietas* really refers to is dutifulness toward parents, native country, and God. The commandment "Honor your father and your mother," therefore, teaches more than obedience to parents. It summons us to love our brothers and sisters, our fellow countrymen, our neighbors, all those with

whom we have some social or racial bond (see
Leviticus 19:17-18). It is the law of blood loyalty, of
tribal cohesion, of adherence to the religion and gods
of one's people. To "honor your father and your
mother" means to be loyal to the attitudes, values,
customs, laws and practices of one's family, tribe and
nation. It is the law of blood relationship. It comes
out of the primeval cry common to animals and men
alike: "We are one blood, ye and I!"[1]

The Leviticus teaching, "Love your neighbor as
yourself" is essentially the same law. That is why
Jesus can join the two commandments together in His
list. The "neighbor" in the minds of those who lived
before Jesus was the man or woman with whom one
had some bond of relationship. So what both of these
commandments are saying to us is, "Love your
brother, your sister, your fellow countryman; be loyal
to your friends, to your family, to your own kind."
What they do not tell us is to love the stranger with
whom we have no racial or family bond. This is what
makes the story of the Good Samaritan so significant
(see *Luke* 10:25-37). The Jews of Samaria and the
Jews of Judea were at odds with one another; they
were enemies. But the Samaritan, who was not a
"neighbor" as the people of Jesus' time understood
the word, showed himself a neighbor to the stranger
he found in need.

It makes sense, therefore, that Jesus should join
together as a summary and climax of all the commandments which treat of our relationship with
others these two: "Honor your father and mother,"
and "Love your neighbor as yourself." They are the
foundation of human community, the ground on
which all natural societies are built.

The community into which Jesus calls us, however, is more than human. It is not a natural society, but a sharing in the life of God. For this reason the most fundamental law of human society has got to be rewritten. Jesus retains the teaching "Love your neighbor as yourself" (see *Matthew* 23:39), but He changes the meaning of the terms. He reaffirms the love that is based on family and tribal bonds, but He gives a new extension to family and tribe. For those who are reborn in grace, even enemies are family. This is His new teaching in the next passage that we take up in the Sermon on the Mount (*Matthew* 5:43-48).

When Jesus cites the old law as being "love your countryman but hate your enemy" (*Matthew* 5:43) He is simply recalling what we spontaneously tend to do as human beings. (The Old Testament did call people to love their neighbor; it said nothing about hating one's enemies). To "hate" one's enemy, as the word is used here, does not mean to actively dislike or attack him. It just means to own no bond of relationship with him, to leave him outside of one's circle of concern. In this sense we "hate" anyone whose needs we have no impulse to answer. To put "America first," for example, in such a way that in our national and business policies we simply do not bother to listen to the cries of hunger and oppression throughout the rest of the world would be to live by this old law. And it is a very natural thing to do.

The new law of Jesus is, "Love your enemies, pray for your persecutors" (*Matthew* 5:44). This law, like all the others Jesus teaches, is not a law which commands specific actions so much as it is a law of interior conversion. What the law really summons us to do is change our minds about the relationship we presume we have — or do not have — with those who are "outsiders" or even positively hostile to us. What Jesus is really saying is that, for those who have been reborn by grace to be "sons of your heavenly Father," all men are to be looked upon as brothers.

For God the artificial divisions of nationality and social class do not exist. Nor does His love make any distinction between people according to the divisions of race and family. God loves all men and women for what they are — and even more so for what they can be — and He does not base His love in any way upon the categories they fall into. The reason for this is that God is related directly, immediately and intimately with every human being on earth through His own act of bringing each one into existence. We are all the work of His hands — and the beloved objects of His heart — and no race, class or family is more dear to Him than any other, because He is not any more the Creator of one group than He is of any other.

If we are "sons of the Father" — that is, if we share in God's own life in the only way that this is possible, by being incorporated into the Body of Christ as "sons in the Son" — then we have to love as God does. And this means we have to love all human beings without distinction, just as God does.

This love must include the bad as well as the good. God does not stop loving people because they sin. Jesus points out that the Father causes the sun to rise on the bad as well as on the good, and sends rain equally to the just and the unjust (*Matthew* 5:45). In other words, God is pure benevolence to all of His creatures, and He does not withhold His favor or His help from people because they sin. On the contrary, as Jesus will also point out later in the parable of the shepherd, He will leave the ninety-nine faithful sheep out on the hills and "go in search of the stray" (*Matthew* 18:12-14). From His side God does not have enemies. He is nothing but love for all men, and He goes out to each one in kindness and compassion according to each one's need.

Jesus gives this same teaching in story form in the parable of the good Samaritan (see *Luke* 10:25-37). There the question is precisely the same as the one we have been discussing: "Who is my neighbor?" To whom must I give the love the commandment calls for? The answer Jesus gives erases the distinction — and the hostility that existed — between the Jews of Judea and those of Samaria. The "neighbor" is anyone in need, and that means every human being who exists. We accept to be neighbors to others when, with compassion, we respond to their needs as to our own.

The teaching of Jesus, then, is that we simply have to erase any distinction that remains in our minds between "us" and "them" — whatever may be the grounds for the distinction. Because we are reborn in grace, because we are children of the Father, all men are brothers to us, all women are our sisters. As St. Paul will later express it: "Each one of you is a son of God because of your faith in Christ Jesus. All of you who have been baptized into Christ have clothed yourselves with him. There does not exist among you Jew or Greek, slave or freeman, male or female. All are one in Christ Jesus" (*Galatians* 3:26-28).

If this is what we are, then this is the way we must love one another.

In proclaiming this new law of universal love, Jesus is also proclaiming the good news of grace. The commandment in Exodus: "Honor your father and your mother," was followed by a promise: "that you may have a long life in the land which the LORD, your God, is giving you" (*Exodus* 20:12). The commandment Jesus gives us is followed by the same promise; only, instead of a "long life" the reward is eternal life. The only way we can love as the Father loves is to participate as sharers in the Father's own act of loving. This means sharing in the life of God. If we are commanded to love as God loves, therefore, we must be offered a share in His life. And since God's life is without beginning or end, we who share in His life possess life that is eternal.

This section (5:43-48) of the Sermon on the Mount ends with the summary statement, "In a word, you must be made perfect as your heavenly Father is perfect." That says it all. This is the good news Jesus came to announce, and all His reinterpretation of the Ten Commandments comes down to saying this: that we are invited now to share in the life of God by grace, and that this divine life which is given to us will be our beatifying joy forever. The new law of Jesus is simply a law of interior conversion that calls us to be like God. The teachings of Jesus are not based on what is natural and good for human beings, but on what is natural and proper to God. The goal of His law is neither good behavior alone nor the good human life on earth. The goal of Jesus' law is union of mind and heart with God. That is why it is a law, not for Pharisees and legalists, and not even for obedient servants. It is a law for disciples; and only those can follow it who are willing to study the mind and heart of God as revealed in the person of Jesus.

His law is a journey of the heart.

FOOTNOTE

[1] See Rudyard Kipling, THE JUNGLE BOOK.

CHAPTER EIGHT: HONOR YOUR FATHER, YOUR FOE —
Matthew 5:43-48

Summary:

1. The commandments "Honor your father and your mother," and "Love your neighbor as yourself" belong together. Both are telling us, in the Old Testament understanding of the terms, to be loyal and supportive toward all those with whom we have some natural bond of family, race, nationality, or social grouping. They are the law of *pietas,* of blood loyalty, of tribal cohesion, on which all human society is built. Jesus uses them to summarize all the commandments which tell us how to deal with other people (see *Matthew* 19:17-19).

2. Jesus calls us to transcend this natural law of family and tribal bonding. He opens to us a new perspective, that of the new and supernatural bonding of grace. Because God calls us to share in His own life by grace, we can now call God our Father, and we must look upon all men and women on earth as our brothers and sisters in Christ. This relationship becomes real when a person is reborn by grace into the family of God; but since all are called to this we must, for practical purposes, love everyone with the love of brother or sister. This is the only way to love as our heavenly Father does and to show that we are truly His children.

3. To "hate your enemy," as it appears in the principle Jesus rejects, does not mean to be actively hostile toward anyone. It simply means to leave some people — those with whom one has no natural bond of relationship — out of one's circle of concern; to look upon their needs and difficulties as something one has no call to be involved in. We fall short of Jesus' teaching whenever we let the artificial divisions of race, nationality or social class diminish our sense of solidarity with other people.

4. God does not withhold His favors or benevolence from those who sin. He gives Himself to all people constantly, in whatever measure they are open or willing to receive Him, without holding their offenses against them, just as He lets His sun shine and His rain fall equally on all. Jesus calls on us to do the same.

Questions for prayer and discussion:

1. If I were going to make a list of the people or groups I think of as being "us" as opposed to "them," what would I write down? What would I do for my family and closest friends

that I wouldn't do for anyone else? What would change in my attitude if I began seriously to consider the whole human race as my family?

2. What does it mean to say we are "brothers and sisters in Christ?" What do blood brothers and sisters have in common? What do the children of God have in common? There is an expression: "Blood is thicker than water." Which is a closer relationship in reality: the bond of blood, or the bond we have through the waters of baptism? Why?

3. What people or groups of people are there whose needs, for all practical purposes, I am indifferent to? Is there any realistic way in which I could act toward them more as a brother or sister? Do I think my country's foreign policy is consistent with a Christian view of the community of mankind?

4. Do I hold back favors and services from people whose behavior I don't approve of? Why? Does God? Am I just as willing to do everything I can do for a person who has offended me as I am for someone who is nice to me? In what concrete ways in my life can I begin to be more like God in this?

CHAPTER NINE

MAKE ME A SABBATH OF YOUR HEART
The Freedom to Face Upwards

The Ten Commandments begin with the precepts that tell us how to relate to God — "I, the LORD, am your God. You shall not have other gods besides me . . . You shall not take the name of the LORD, your God, in vain . . . Remember to keep holy the sabbath day?" They continue with the commandments that tell us how to act toward other people: "Honor your father and your mother . . . you shall not kill, commit adultery, steal, bear false witness against your neighbor, covet your neighbor's goods or his wife."

In the Sermon on the Mount, Jesus comments first on the commandments which tell us how to deal with other people. He transforms these from laws defining good human behavior to laws that teach us to be one in heart and mind and life with God Himself.

Now, in chapter six of Matthew, Jesus takes up the commandments which govern our relationship with God. In His instruction on these commandments, Jesus will not focus on concrete actions which we are to perform or not perform; His focus will be on our attitude of heart. He will teach us through these commandments what our interior stance of mind and heart and soul toward God should be.

Our natural human tendency is to turn everything God says into limited, particular rules. We take God's first commandment to be just a prohibition of idol-worship, spiritualism, and superstitious practices. We take the commandment against using His name in vain to be just a rule against cursing or dishonest oaths. And we take the commandment about the sabbath day to be no more than a rule about going to church and not working on Sundays.

The truth is that these commandments, taken all together, constitute a profound teaching on the nature of God and of man's relationship to God. And this is what the teaching of Jesus will bring out. But Jesus will also flavor His teaching with a strong, if implicit, revelation of the new relationship we are called to have with God through grace. This is the real "good news" of His explanation.

Jesus begins with the commandment "Remember to keep holy the sabbath day" and works backward to "you shall not have other gods besides me."

Jesus doesn't actually mention the sabbath observance at all in His Sermon on the Mount. The reason for this may be that Matthew will show Jesus later on battling the Pharisees precisely over the question of the sabbath observance, and His interpretation as opposed to theirs will be a touchstone of true Christian belief (see *Matthew* 12:6,8,14). The sabbath, and sabbath-day observance, was, together with the temple in Jerusalem, the most visible symbol of orthodox Judaism. For the Pharisees, to violate the sabbath was to reject the whole Jewish law and the Covenant. To speak against the temple and its central place in Jewish worship was to attack Judaism at its heart (see *Matthew* 26:61; *John* 2:18-22 and 4:19-26; *Acts* 4:11 and 6:13,48-49). This is what made Jesus so threatening to the Pharisees: He came proclaiming Himself Lord even of the sabbath (*Matthew* 12:8) and making His own body the focus of Christian worship instead of the temple (see *John* 2:19). A transcendence of the sabbath, therefore, is implicit throughout Matthew's whole Gospel. It is no longer the law of sabbath observance which is the sign of the holiness to which God calls His people (see *Exodus* 31:13) but the doctrine of the risen Body of Christ made visible in His Church (see *Matthew* 12:39 and 16:4). The temple, too, has been replaced by the living Body of Christ; that is, by the Church enlivened and enlightened by the Spirit of Christ (see *John* 4:23-24). And circumcision, which was the mark of the covenant between God and Abraham (see *Genesis* 17:9-12) is replaced by baptism, through which we enter into the death of Christ, die with Him, and rise again as members of the Church to live as His Body on earth (see *Colossians* 2:1 to 3:11). With Jesus the focus shifts from the sabbaths as a sign of man's relationship with God to Jesus Himself and to His Church as God's living, continuing presence among men.

Jesus doesn't take up the law of sabbath observance directly in the Sermon on the Mount. But He does single out for commentary the three traditional Jewish expressions of devotion to God: almsgiving, prayer and fasting (see *Matthew* 6:1-18). In elevating our understanding of these He raises our understanding of the sabbath to a new and transcendent height.

Jesus doesn't abolish these practices. Even today, prayer, fasting and compassion toward the poor are basic expressions of the spiritual life, and they always will be. But Jesus uses these examples to teach that religion cannot be just a matter of cultural identification. One isn't devout because it contributes to Jewish (or Irish) nationalism, and one isn't a Christian because it is the "American" thing to be. There is only one reason to perform any religious act, and that is God. To engage in expressions of devotion for any other reason — to fit in with one's culture, to please one's family, to make a good impression on a boy or girl one would like to date, or because it creates a good public image for one's business — this is false worship. To be a "churchgoer" because it is an act of insertion into the local community is not true devotion to God. It violates the very meaning and message of the sabbath.

The reason for the sabbath rest was not just to give people time for worship. The sabbath observance was essentially a teaching device: God insisted that His People take one day off a week in order to center them on Himself rather than on this world. And "this world" includes the people in it.

The word "sabbath" means "leisure". The real law of the sabbath was not that people should go to church, but that they should do no work that day. By taking a day off, a day of leisure, man expresses the fact that he is different from everything else in the universe; that he has and is called to a special relationship with God. A book for Jewish school children explains this very beautifully:

"The Shabbat marks the difference between man and all other creatures that live in the universe; the Shabbat celebrates the tie between God and the Jews.

"Man is different from everything else in nature. He is different from the animals of the land and sea;

different from the trees and grasses that grow in
earth; different from the seas and mountains that
cover the earth.

"Nothing interferes with the regular rhythm of nature
— except man. The sun rises and sets each day,
without stop. The moon comes up, grows, gets small,
and disappears every 29 days, without stop. The tides
fill and the tides ebb, without stop. The grass comes
up every spring; the trees bear fruit every fall, without
halt. Only death stops the regular rhythm of natural
things — but death, too, is part of the unending circle
of life.

"But man can and does stop his work, stop his
running, stop following his animal instincts. He stops
even though his work isn't finished, even though there
is more he wants to do. He rests, he thinks. He looks
back on what he has won, which other creatures do
not do. He looks ahead, as animals and trees cannot;
he chooses the way he will go. He thanks God for
all His help and asks God for continuing help in
choosing wisely.

"He does this on the Shabbat. The Shabbat is the
greatest of holidays because then man becomes truly
a man, different from all the animals."[1]

Man is different from the rest of creation because
he can think and understand; because he has freedom
and can choose. But most of all he is different
because, being rational, he is by his very nature called
to a special relationship with God.

Everything else in the universe exists for one
reason only: to contribute to the functioning and life
of the whole. The minerals, plants, animals, stars and
seasons have no reason to exist outside of this world;
they have no meaning, no value, no *raison-d-etre*
except to do their part in keeping the universe going.
But this is not true of man.

Man, because he has an intellect, can know there

is a God. Because he has a will he can worship God; he can appreciate and love what he understands. He can adore. This is something that belongs to the very nature of man as such; it is what it means to be a human being. And it is because of this special, this direct relationship with God that man can never look upon himself or any human person as being just another cog in the gears of the universe, nor as a slave to the state or to the culture.

The inalienable rights of the human person come from this, that each one was created, not just to contribute to society or to the world, but to know and adore God. Therefore society can never treat individual human beings as if they had no value except in terms of their contribution to society. The government cannot regulate people's lives as if they had nothing to live for except the good of the state. The unanimous vote of the whole human race is not enough to take away the rights of one single human being, because people do not exist solely for one another or for the world but for God. This is why no dictator, congress, or court has the right to legislate away the lives of the unborn, or allow the extermination of the weak, the old, the helpless, the unfit. This is also why no government can deny to any human being the free judgment of his conscience in matters of religion. If man has a reason for existing that is outside of this world, then no value within the world can claim man entirely for itself. This is the lesson of sabbath-day observance. It is an emancipation proclamation.

The sabbath teaches us our difference from the rest of creation by requiring us, one day a week, to act in a way that is different from the rest of nature. On the sabbath we simply stop doing whatever work we do to keep the world going around. "Work" is defined as anything a person does just because it has to get done. And one day a week God tells us not to do any work, just so we can learn through the experience (and keep aware of it) that we have a reason for existing — and a value as persons — which has nothing to do with what we contribute to the smooth functioning of the universe. The sabbath is a teaching device; it teaches us where our true center is: not in this world, but in God.[2]

In the Sermon on the Mount, Jesus shows how the spirit behind the sabbath observance should apply to all of our religious acts. If God is our center, then all of our acts of devotion should be directed to Him alone. Almsgiving, prayer, fasting: these are not to be performed for the sake of winning favor from men, but solely for the sake of pleasing God (see *Matthew* 6:1-18).

What Jesus is emphasizing here is that religious acts are not something one engages in just because one is a member of a community. They are not for the sake of human relationships. Nor are they just a duty to society. Acts of religion are not another form of "work," through which each member of society pays his dues to God in order to keep God favorable to the community. They can easily be understood this way, however, and they have been in the past.

In a society such as Israel, in which church and state were united, and the good of the People depended on their fidelity to their Covenant with God (see, for example, *Deuteronomy,* ch. 8), there was danger that the individual might lose sight of personal relationship with God while being faithful to all the religious observances of the People. To be devout was to be a good Jew; and to be a good Jew was to be an asset rather than a liability to society. Therefore to show one's devotion in public was an expression of patriotism. This is why Jesus had to put weight on the other side of the balance.

Jesus recognized the need for public expressions of religion. He Himself worshipped in the synagogue with other people (see *Matthew* 12:9; 13:54). When He cured a leper He sent him to fulfill the proper ritual with the priest (*Matthew* 8:4). His own followers continued to go to the temple to pray in the days following Pentecost (see *Acts* 2:46; 3:1; and 21:26). But if every religious act one does is done in public, or as part of the community's formal worship, it is easy to lose sight of one's own personal relationship with God. Faith then can degenerate into just cultural identification, and religion can be more a matter of loyalty to family and social group than it is devotion to God.

The meaning behind the law of sabbath observance is that man is called to immediate relationship with God. Human beings are called, not just to do practical things on earth, but above all to express themselves to God, and to recognize God's expression of Himself to them. This is what religious observances should be: acts of personal self-expression to God. Acts of devotion, however, such as prayer, fasting and almsgiving, are in constant danger of becoming just "acts of religion" — that is, just practices, pious routines, something one "does" because one is a member of a church. The soul goes out of religious acts when they become just elements of a system instead of personal expressions of the heart to God.

Jesus teaches that the value of religious acts lies, not in what is done, or even in the fact that certain things are done, but in the response of mind and will and heart to God that these actions express. The value of our religious response to God is not measured by how many prayers we say (see *Matthew* 6:7); by how much money we contribute (see *Luke* 21:1-4); or by how frequently we fast (see *Matthew* 8:14-17), but simply by the love, the faith, the hope, the generosity that our actions sincerely express. Prayers, fasting, almsgiving are simply the form we give to something we are trying to say to God; and it is what we intend to say through these actions — and say precisely to God, not to anyone else — which gives them their value.

That is why Jesus teaches in the Sermon on the Mount: "In giving alms you are not to let your left hand know what your right hand is doing. Keep your deeds of mercy secret . . . " And, "when you pray, go to your room, close the door, and pray to your Father in private." In the same way, "when you fast, see to it that you groom your hair and wash your face. In that way no one can see you are fasting but your Father . . . "

The way to know that we are acting for God alone — and that God is real to us, that we believe in Him — is to set up a "nothing but" situation. When the motive for our action can be "nothing but" God, we know we are acting for Him. And the way to achieve "nothing-butness" — and through this the experience of personal relationship with God — is to remove every other possible motive for what we are doing. That is why Jesus says to give alms secretly, pray in secret, and fast without anyone's knowing it. When we have taken pains to make sure we receive no recompense on earth for what we do, we know we believe in the reward that comes from God. When we perform religious acts in a way that cannot be seen by men, we become more and more conscious of our personal relationship with a God who sees and who cares.

There is something different about the God Jesus pictures to us here. He is not just the God of the community, the God of the Covenant who has chosen to enter into relationship with one particular nation, and therefore indirectly with every member of it. The God Jesus speaks of He calls "your Father." He is a close and intimate God, a Father who "sees in secret"; who "sees what no man sees," who "sees what is hidden" (*Matthew* 6:4,6,18). This is a God who sees the secret attitudes and inclinations of the heart, because He dwells in our hearts. And Jesus teaches us here to relate to Him, not just through our public actions as members of a community, but above all through the personal interior response of our minds and hearts and wills to Him.

It is the "flavor" of our Lord's words here, rather than their actual content, which suggests the God of grace. God is our Father. He is close and intimately present to each one of us. He is a God who sees and rewards the response of our hearts to Him. He is not just the God who can be known through the intellect by any rational creature, the God all human beings are equipped by nature to adore. He is a God who communicates Himself intimately to man. In calling us to focus our devotional practices on this God, Jesus is preparing us for the revelation of the gift of grace.

In practical terms, what lesson do we draw from this section of the Sermon on the Mount? In the passages we are considering (*Matthew* 6:1-18), Jesus really says only one thing: that in our acts of almsgiving, prayer and fasting we should act, not for men, but for God alone. What is He teaching us through this?

The first thing is that we should look upon these acts of devotion, not in the first place as things that must be *done* — that is, as part of the "work" of being devout — but primarily and essentially as *expressions of the heart*.

In chapter nine of Matthew's Gospel the disciples of John the Baptizer raise the objection with Jesus: "Why is it that while we and the Pharisees fast, your disciples do not?" For them fasting was an "exercise" of the spiritual life, and everyone had to *do* it to be holy. Jesus answers by telling them that fasting is essentially an act of *self-expression:* What are they trying to *say* (not do) when they fast? "How can wedding guests go in mourning so long as the groom is with them? When the day comes that the groom is taken away, then they will fast" (*Matthew* 9:14-15). Fasting is a way of expressing the hunger of one's heart for God; it is a chosen, physical state of hunger that gives body to the recognized, spiritual hunger of one's soul for union with God, for the "wedding feast" (see also *Psalms* 42 and 84). Naturally, while the disciples were enjoying the consolation of the physical presence of Jesus, they could not fast.

In His teaching about religion Jesus puts the emphasis, not on what we do, but on the interior attitudes of mind and heart and will that are being expressed by what we do. In doing this He calls us, not to obedience only, and not to the observance of a set of practices which constitute some "system" of devotion; He calls us to discipleship — that is, to a modeling of our hearts and minds on His own. This is a religion of deeply personal relationship with God.[3]

The second thing Jesus is teaching here is that we are made for relationship with God. This is not just the relationship we are able to establish through intellect and will — that is, through the fact of being rational creatures who can understand and adore. He calls us to a relationship more intimate than that: the relationship of grace.

The sabbath-day observance was a way of teaching God's People that as human beings they were different from all other creatures on earth. And God entered into a special Covenant with the Jews. This made them holy, a "people set apart" (*Leviticus* 20:22-26) and laid on them the privileged obligation to "be holy because I, your God, am holy" (see *Leviticus* 11:45). But what God asked of His People in that Covenant was essentially just that they should live good human lives according to the laws He taught them, and on top of this, believe in Him and in His promises to them. And the People did not understand those promises to include much more than the well-being of the community as such, and a long and happy life on earth for its faithful members.

In the Sermon on the Mount, however, Jesus changes the terms of the Covenant. We have already seen how He reinterpreted the commandments that deal with our relationship toward other men. He transformed the Ten Commandments from a set of laws prescribing good, human behavior into a summons to think and to love like God Himself. He also started His listeners thinking in terms of reward and punishment after death, and in this way prepared them for the revelation of everlasting life: that God Himself will be our beatitude forever (see chapter three above). This was already an implicit revelation of grace.

Now, when Jesus teaches us to perform our acts of devotion — our almsgiving, prayer and fasting — for God's eyes alone, He is taking us one step deeper into this revelation. Not only is the community of Israel a chosen people, a people set apart, but so, in a particular, personal way, is every individual in it. When Jesus tells us to pray to our Father in secret, He is calling attention to the close, personal relationship which the Father has with each and every believer. We are not made holy just because we belong to a people whom God has set apart for Himself. Each one of us is holy in a deeper, more personal, more intimate and mysterious way. What is this way?

It is the divine indwelling. The People of God were holy because God dwelt in their midst in a special way.[4] Now each individual Christian is holy because the Three Persons of the Trinity come to "make their dwelling place" within each one's heart (see *John* 14:23; 15:4). The sabbaths were a sign of the holiness to which God's People were called. They were a reminder of His abiding presence among them. But Jesus has made the holiness we experience — the indwelling, sanctifying presence of the Spirit in our hearts — a sign of the sabbath to which we are called. This is the "eternal sabbath" of heaven to which all of us are called as children of the Father and members of the risen Jesus. This "eternal sabbath" is our sharing in the personal life of God (see *Galatians* 3:2,4; and *Romans* 8:14-27; 1 *John* 4:13 and 5:6).

"In six days," the Scripture tells us, "the LORD made the heavens and the earth, the sea and all that is in them; but on the seventh day he rested." The meaning of this is that God has an existence of His own apart from this world. He is not just some kind of primal force which keeps the universe in motion.

The world is not God's reason for being; He created the world because He wanted to, but being Creator is not His whole life; He has other things to do, a personal life of His own. There is more to God — and therefore more to reality — than just the life and activity of this world. That is what the Scripture means by telling us God took a "day off." And by telling His People to take a day off from the world too, God taught them that they, like Himself, are not simply identified with this world. There is more to man's life — more experience open to him — than just his experience of this world. "That is why," the Scripture continues, "the LORD blessed the sabbath day and made it holy" (see *Exodus* 20:11). The sabbath reminds us that we, like God, are called to a life apart from and beyond this world.

When Jesus promised the gift of the Holy Spirit at the Last Supper (*John* 14:23-26), He said at the same time that His followers would never be "of the world" (*John* 15:18 ff.). Here He means more than the distinction between rational, free human beings and the rest of creation. He means that between His followers and human society, human culture, there will always be tension and conflict. Christianity is a centrifugal force in the world: the center for Christians is outside of this world; it is in God. Human culture, on the other hand, is spontaneously centripetal with regard to this world; it tends to locate its center in the world itself and to become enclosed in the values and priorities of this world alone. Hence there is opposition between the world-transcending, God centered direction of Christianity and the world-centered, God-excluding tendency of human cultures.[5] At the most, human cultures recognize God and accept Him as establishing boundaries, but do not center on Him.

For that reason Jesus says to His followers, at the same time that He promises the gift of the Holy Spirit and the gift of the Trinity's divine indwelling:

> If you belonged to the world,
> it would love you as its own;
> the reason it hates you
> is that you do not belong to the world.
> But I chose you out of the world.   (*John* 15:19)

The "holiness" of Christians consists, not only in our being different from the rest of creation through endowment with intellect and will which make us able to adore; nor does it come only from the fact that God has chosen to make us His own People, to dwell in our midst, instruct us and guide our history, "setting us apart" for His own purposes, to be His special People and the instrument of His saving work on earth. The holiness, the consecration, the sanctification of Christians consists primarily and above all in the gift of God's indwelling presence in our hearts. God Himself has chosen to become the center of our every thought, decision and desire. God has given us Himself in the intimate closeness of the union He has with each one of us by grace. Now God not only dwells and acts in the midst of His People, but He dwells in each one of us, in each member of the Body of Christ, as in His own temple: we are, each one of us, individually as well as collectively, the "temple of the Holy Spirit" (see 1 *Corinthians* 6:19 and 3:16-17). The sign of the sabbath has been transcended. God Himself is our sabbath. He is the holiness and everlasting leisure of our souls. He has called us to share in His own personal life, in the life He lives apart from the world, the life the Scripture refers to when it says, "on the seventh day God rested." God's own life is our eternal rest, and we enter into this rest through faith and reflection on His indwelling word (see *Hebrews* 4:1-12), and through the experience of His Spirit within us. The "sabbath day" for Christians in this world is discipleship of the heart.

FOOTNOTES

[1] From *When A Jew Celebrates*, by Harry Gersh (Behrman House Inc., 1971) pp. 83-84.

[2] The meaning of the sabbath as an expression of emancipation from this world is developed in my book *Lift Up Your Eyes To The Mountain*, Dimension Books, 1981, chapter 5: "A People Set Apart — Christian Separation From The World."

[3] For an explanation of how Jesus' teaching on fasting is also a revelation of grace, see *Why Jesus?*, ch. 13, pp. 144-146.

[4] See *Dictionary of Biblical Theology*, ed. Xavier Leon-Dufour; tr. P. Joseph Cahill (Desclee, 1973), under "holy."

[5] For a development of this, and for the way that Christians achieve holiness *within* the world, by renewing human society and its institutions in the spirit of the Gospel, see my books *His Way*, chapters 10 and 11 (St. Anthony Messenger Press, 1977) and *Lift Up Your Eyes To The Mountain*, chapter 7 (Dimension Books, 1981).

CHAPTER NINE: MAKE ME A SABBATH OF YOUR HEART — *Matthew* 6:1-8; 16-18

Summary:

1. In chapter six Matthew shows Jesus taking up the commandments which govern our relationship with God (as opposed to those which govern our relationship with other people). And as with the other commandments, the teaching of Jesus here does not focus on concrete actions or particular rules of behavior, but on the attitude of mind and heart which we should develop within ourselves and express externally in our actions. This is a very profound attitude of personal, graced relationship with God.

2. Jesus does not take up directly in the Sermon on the Mount the commandment "Remember to keep holy the sabbath day;" but He does take up the traditional Jewish expressions of devotion: almsgiving, prayer and fasting. He shifts the

emphasis in these acts away from public expression of relationship with others through participation in the life and religion of Israel and toward personal expression of relationship with God. Jesus tells us to pray and fast "in secret" because acts performed in secret can have no meaning or value except as acts of personal expression to God. As such they are not only an expression but an experience of one's faith that God is present and attentive to one's actions, and of one's personal desire to acknowledge His place in one's life.

3. Jesus' teaching here does bring the law of sabbath observance to its fulfillment. The sabbath leisure is meant to teach us (as it taught the Jews) our special relationship with God. To stop working one day a week is a way of saying — and therefore of realizing — that we have a reason for existing and a purpose in life which is distinct from what we do in and for this world. We have an immediate relationship with God. We exist to know Him, to love Him and to serve Him with praise, reverence and thanksgiving and no relationship with or obligation to other human beings can take priority over this.

4. The teaching of Jesus emphasizes that religious acts themselves are not another form of "work," something we just do as members of a community, to keep the community pleasing to God, or because they are part of the "system" we belong to. They are acts of personal interaction with the Lord. The value of our religious acts comes, not from what is done, but from what they express. Fasting, prayer and almsgiving mean nothing except as authentic expressions of personal faith, hope and love. They are pleasing to God, not as routines, but as the form we give to something we want to say to God. Understood as such, they help us to grow in awareness of God as seeing, caring, close, intimate, and communicating Himself to us by grace.

5. What Jesus is really doing here is introducing us — through the "tone" rather than through the content of what He says — to that intimate, special relationship which we have with God through grace. In the Old Testament the sabbaths were a sign of the holiness to which God's people were called. In Christianity the holiness poured out in our hearts through grace is a sign of the "eternal sabbath" to which we are invited. Our graced intimacy with the indwelling God in our hearts is a foretaste and pledge of the eternal, perfect sharing in God's own life in heaven which is our destiny. This destiny alone is the key which allows us to understand the purpose and value of human life on earth, and the way people

experience their existence. We are in the world, but we are called and destined to apartness. That apartness is the life of God Himself, which was before the world was created and which infinitely transcends it. That life is our destiny, and even while we work and live on earth, it is not the world or what we do in it, but our call to union with God beyond this world which gives the key to our existence.

Questions for prayers and discussion:

1. What acts of devotion do I do that are just between myself and God? Do I have times of personal prayer that are not just what is "expected" of everybody in my religion? How do I pray at these times? Do I experience these moments as something very personal between myself and God? Do I experience them as acts of my own free choice? In them do I become aware of my faith as something unique and personal to myself, and not just something which I have as a member of a particular religious group?

2. Is there any real day of leisure in my week? Do I observe the "sabbath" (leisure day) consciously as a way of saying to myself and to God that I am free to "let the world go by" one day a week? Does the sabbath increase my awareness that I am made for God and for relationship with Him, and that everything I do in this world is secondary? Why is just "taking off" one day a week a way of saying and of realizing this?

3. In my religious acts — of prayer and worship, of "fasting" under any form (sacrifices for God, acts of self-denial or of penance), of almsgiving (generosity to the poor, tithing, contributions to good causes, etc.) — am I primarily aware of what I am saying to God? Or do I look upon these acts mostly as duties to perform, obligations to meet, acts whose value lies in what they effect rather than in what they express?

4. How did the sabbath observance remind the Jews of God's own apartness from (transcendence of) the world? How does the indwelling presence of God in our hearts by grace remind us of our own call to enter into and to share the personal life of God forever in heaven? Do I experience this indwelling in any way? How?

CHAPTER TEN

PRAY: "FATHER . . . KINGDOM . . . COME!"
(The God of Intimacy and Hope)

On Mount Sinai God warned His People: "You shall not take the name of the LORD, your God, in vain." Now Jesus, speaking also on a mountainside, teaches us to pray, "Our Father, . . . hallowed be thy name!" With this teaching He lifts our attitude toward God to another plane entirely and brings the commandment of Sinai to fulfillment.

The setting is the same, yet different. Matthew presents Jesus going "up on the mountainside" (*Matthew* 5:1), just as Moses went up to the top of Mount Sinai (*Exodus* 19:20). But when God spoke on Sinai, the people were not allowed to approach. "Set limits for the people all around the mountain," God said to Moses, "and tell them: Take care not to go up to the mountain, or even to touch its base. If anyone touches the mountain he must be put to death." When God gave the law on Sinai, He came in thunder and lightning. Mount Sinai was wrapped in fire and smoke; a cloud covered its peak and the whole mountain shook (*Exodus* 19:12-19).

When Jesus taught on the mountainside, however, He simply sat down and called His disciples to gather around Him. Then He began to teach them (*Matthew* 5:1-2).

The contrast is deliberate. It marks a change in man's relationship with God. God is no longer distant, terrifying and unapproachable. The closeness and intimacy which began after Yahweh revealed His name to Moses (see *Exodus* 3:13 ff. and WHY JESUS?, chapter 1) is brought to completion in Jesus. And in the framework of Scriptural thought, this change of relationship calls for a change of name.[1]

Jesus gave God a new name for us when He taught us to pray, "Our Father . . . " (*Matthew* 6:9 ff.) And in this prayer He transforms and brings to its fulfillment the commandment given on Sinai: "You shall not take the name of the LORD, your God, in vain. For the Lord will not leave unpunished him who takes his name in vain" (*Exodus* 20:7).

On Sinai the commandment was given with a threat; and in Jewish law blasphemy against the name of God was punishable by death (see *Leviticus* 24:10-16). The purpose of the commandment was to teach reverence, respect for the transcendent majesty of God. The object of Jesus' new teaching, however, is to teach intimacy, a family relationship with God, "familiarity" in the root sense of the word. And this is a familiarity that is only made possible by grace.

We are able to call God "Father" with the familiarity of sons only because we are sons — sons and daughters of the Father through incorporation into the Body of Christ who is the "only-begotten Son of God." We are *"filii in Filio,"* "sons in the Son," because Jesus Christ has brought us by baptism into the unity of His own Body and shared His Spirit and His life with us. All this is the new relationship with God which we recall when we say, "Our Father . . . "

When He renews the Ten Commandments in the Sermon on the Mount, Jesus does not just forbid all irreverence for God's name. Instead He teaches us to pray in a positive sense, "Hallowed be thy name!"

This prayer is not just a human desire. It is not just the preference any human being might have that God be given due reverence on earth. When the Christian prays, "Hallowed be thy name!", this is a cry of wonder, of praise and of love that wells up from within him, out of the mystery of his graced knowledge of God. It is a "breadth and length and height and depth" of desire which only those can have who know God as God knows Himself. It is a cry of identification with God in the knowledge God has of His own name. And this identification comes from the fact that within the hearts of those who are blessed with the indwelling presence of God by grace the Holy Spirit Himself is crying out the name of God with an eloquence greater than words (see *Matthew* 11:27; *Galatians* 4:6; 1 *Corinthians* 12:3; *Philippians* 2:9-11). When we pray "Our Father," the Spirit within us is crying out "Abba! Father!" just as He cries out within us, "Jesus is Lord!"

When Christians pray, "Hallowed be thy name!" they are already joined on earth to the chorus which the blessed in heaven are crying out day and night before the unveiled majesty of God:

"Holy, holy, holy is the Lord God
  Almighty,
He who was, and who is, and who
  is to come!"   (*Revelation* 4:8)

"Hallowed be thy name!" expresses an identification of *mind* with God: we are able to speak the name of God as God Himself speaks it, because the Holy Spirit is revealing this name within our hearts. This is the gift of faith.

The next two petitions of the Our Father express the identification of our *wills* with the will of God. "Thy Kingdom come! Thy will be done on earth as it is in heaven!" Because we are the Body of Christ, one with Him as the members of a body are one with the head, the mission of Jesus is our mission, and His will to accomplish it is our own driving desire. The New Covenant is not founded, as the Old Covenant was, on an agreement to keep God's law. It is founded on a sharing in God's life through incorporation into the Body of Jesus Christ on earth. And this sharing in His life means that we also embrace His mission, which is to establish the reign of God on earth. When God truly reigns — when His will is done as perfectly on earth as it is in heaven — then the Kingdom will be established (see *Hebrews* 10:1-18 and 1 *Corinthians* 15:22-28). Then all things in heaven and on earth will be brought into one under Christ's headship (see *Ephesians* 1:9-22) and the work of reconciliation will be complete (see *Colossians* 1:15-23). To pray "Thy Kingdom come! Thy will be done!", then, is to profess the total identification of our every will and desire with that of Jesus Christ in the unity of His Body. This is the response of love.

To the revelation of God's beauty and of His loving gift of His own life to us, our minds respond with the cry, "Our Father! Hallowed be thy name!" This is an expression of awestruck faith. To this same revelation our wills respond with a declaration of self-surrendering desire: "Thy Kingdom come! Thy will be done on earth as it is in heaven!" This is a cry of love.

The rest of the Our Father puts the accent on hope.

The whole of the Our Father has been explained as an eschatological prayer.[2] This means it is a prayer which looks forward to, and expresses hope in, the final consummation of redemption in the last days. The "end time" or *eschaton* is that final hour when Christ will come again, the forces of evil will be definitively overcome, and God's reign — His Kingdom — will be complete in all hearts.

According to this interpretation, all the petitions of the Our Father are an expression of hope and desire for the final consummation of all things in Christ. We breathe out the name "Father!" in anticipation of the perfect sonship, the perfect union with God which will be ours in heaven. "Hallowed be thy name!" is an expression of longing for that day when all of creation will be united in adoration of the beauty and holiness of God. "Thy Kingdom come! Thy will be done!" refers to the final realization of God's saving plan, when heaven and earth will be one in surrender to the reign of Christ. But while hope is the inspiration of all the petitions of the Our Father — as are faith and love — it is particularly explicit in the ones that follow.

The petition "Give us this day our daily bread" is one of the most difficult phrases in Scripture to translate. This is because the word rendered here as "daily" — *epiousios* — is not used by any other Greek writer and its meaning is obscure. Father Raymond Brown argues convincingly that the true meaning of this phrase is, "Give us this day the bread of tomorrow" or "our future bread."[3] He refers to the parallel in Exodus, when Moses promises the manna which will come on the *morrow,* but only enough for one day's portion at a time (see *Exodus* 16:4-15); and he points out the linguistic and theological connections between this phrase and other passages in the New Testament which speak of bread (see *John* 6:32, 35, 54 and 1 *Corinthians* 11:26). His conclusion is that the "bread" which we pray for in the Our Father is the bread of the heavenly banquet, of the eternal wedding feast of heaven to which Christ came to call the whole of the human race.

This bread, of course, is Christ Himself (see *John* 6:35); and when Jesus is received in the Eucharist (see 1 *Corinthians* 11:23 ff.) this is a pledge and a foretaste of the eternal union with God which will be ours in heaven.

The bread which we pray for in the Our Father is the same bread, the same Jesus, who will be our delight in heaven and who is given to us on a daily basis here on earth, both in His word and in the Eucharist. In changing the phrase to "Give us this day our daily bread," therefore, the Christian community was not being unfaithful to the meaning of Scripture. She was simply adapting the words of this prayer to daily use in liturgy and personal devotion. Catholics do the same thing when they take the words spoken by the angel and by Elizabeth to Mary in *Luke* 1 (verses 28 and 43) and combine them to form the "Hail Mary."

When Jesus teaches this prayer in the Sermon on the Mount, He is doing more than giving us a beautiful prayer to recite. He is announcing a whole new relationship with God, and teaching us to look forward to a previously undreamed-of destiny. We are called to "eat and drink" with Jesus in His natural home, which is heaven (see *Luke* 22:30). In the image of a meal shared together (see *Revelation* 3:20) Jesus teaches us the union and intimacy with God to which we are called by grace. Not only is the meaning of sabbath-day observance here on earth transcended and transformed by His teaching (see chapter nine above), but the eternal sabbath of man's eschatological destiny is revealed.

Man does not just differ from the rest of creation by nature, because his intellect makes him able to recognize and relate consciously to God (which is what it means to be created "in the image of God": see *Genesis* 1:27); but man is also called to share by grace in the very life and nature of God. This is more than the end — the way of operating — to which man is equipped and ordered by nature. It is the destiny to which he is called and ordered by grace. And in this revelation of man's graced destiny to share in the life and nature of God as true sons and daughters of the Father, gathered around His table as at a family meal, the intention of the sabbath observance is brought to its fulfillment.

A banquet is an image of unity, reconciliation and peace. Only friends and family dine together. And therefore Jesus teaches us to pray for unity and peace among men, which can only be realized when the Father's will is done on earth as perfectly as it is in heaven. Unity and peace can only be brought about through reconciliation, and this is Jesus' mission on earth (see *Ephesians* 1:10; 1 *Corinthians* 15:47-48; *Philippians* 2:19; *Colossians* 1:20). For this reason, at the same time that Jesus instructs us to set our hearts on the "future bread" of the heavenly banquet, He also teaches us to pray: "Forgive us our offenses, as we forgive those who have offended us."

This petition is not directly concerned with the day-to-day forgiveness of day-by-day faults. Its immediate focus is on the final and perfect reconciliation of all things in Christ. It is a prayer which looks forward to that day when there will be no more sinfulness to separate us in any way from God or from one another; when forgiveness will be perfect because our repentance, our conversion of heart and mind to God will be perfect. It is an eschatological prayer. Like the petition before it, it is a cry of hope addressed to God, asking for complete and final redemption.

The last petition of the Our Father — "Lead us not into temptation (or "into hard testing"), but deliver us from evil" — is another cry of hope. The Christian community knows that before the final victory of Christ there will be a struggle to the death with evil. This is true both for the Church as a whole (see *Matthew,* chapter 24; *Revelation,* chapters 8-20) and for each individual person. This petition asks, in the spirit of Jesus' exhortation (see *Matthew* 24:20-22 and 26:41) that this period of conflict will be shortened and made easier.

The Our Father ends, then, on a note of intensified hope, looking to the Father for total deliverance, forgiveness and redemption in the unity of the Kingdom of God.

We can, if we wish, see in the petitions of the Our Father a summary of the teaching Jesus gave on the Ten Commandments as a whole.

To the commandment: "I, the Lord, am your God . . . you shall not have other gods besides me"

Jesus responds, "This is how you are to pray: 'Our Father in heaven . . . '"

To the commandment: "You shall not take the name of the LORD, your God, in vain" He teaches us to pray, "Hallowed be your name!"

The commandment which speaks of man's special relationship with God — "Remember to keep holy the sabbath day" — is transcended in the petitions "Your kingdom come, your will be done on earth as it is in heaven." Man who, alone of all the creatures on earth, is able to consciously conform his will to God's is now called, not just to recognize God's will inscribed in the laws of nature, but to cooperate with Jesus in bringing about the total fulfillment of God's plan — the reconciliation and reestablishment of all things in Christ (see *Ephesians* 1:9 ff. and *Colossians* 1:15 ff.). This is the full revelation of man's call to holiness and of his destiny.

And the law of family love: "Honor your father and your mother, that you may have a long life in the land which the LORD, your God, is giving you" (*Exodus* 20:13) is transcended and given new meaning in the petition "Give us today our bread that is to come."

Our prayer for the "bread of tomorrow" looks forward to the gathering of the whole human race into one family at the banqueting table of the Kingdom — the true Promised Land in which the reward of brotherly love is not just a "long life" but life everlasting (see 1 *John* 3:11 ff.). This petition implies the following one: "Forgive us . . . as we also forgive . . . " because peace and unity among sinful people, or between ourselves and God — the peace of the Kingdom — can only be built on forgiveness.

The last petition: "Subject us not to the trial, but deliver us from the evil one", is concerned, as we have said, with our final struggle, and that of the whole Church, against evil. As such it is concerned above all with fidelity to God in faith, hope and love — with that "persevering to the end" which is the final act of salvation (see *Matthew* 10:22; 24:13). But in daily life our persevering in faith, hope and love takes the form of a constant combat against the evil which threatens to seduce us: "carnal allurements, enticements for the eye, the life of empty show" (1 *John* 2:16). In other words, this last petition returns our attention to life in this world and to the commandments which govern our relationship to the world: You shall not kill, commit adultery, steal, lie, or covet the things of this world.

Christians have made a break, declared themselves emancipated, from the "world" as John uses the term: the cultural environment of this world insofar as it is distorted in its values and direction by sin, closed to the light of Christ, caught up with the "empty show" of short-term, illusory gratifications. This is the "world" of consumerism, of advertisements that manipulate lower appetites in order to create unreasonable, unmeasured desires. It is the world of violence, prejudice, greed, infidelity, lust and head-long ambition. It is this "world" — which is the dark side of the world we live in — that John has in mind when he writes:

> Have no love for the world,
> nor the things that the world affords.
> If anyone loves the world,
> the Father's love has no place in him,
> for nothing that the world affords
> comes from the Father . . .

And the world with its seductions is
  passing away
but the man who does God's will
endures forever.   (1 *John* 2:15-17)
(See also 1 *Peter* 1:13; 2:10; 2 *Peter* 1:4)

The last petition of the Our Father puts us face to
face with the basic choice that confronts every human
being who has heard the good news of Christ: does
one go with the "world" and its passing gratifications, its short-term pleasures and illusory happiness,
or does one "break" with this world and follow the
way of Christ? The way of Christ promises life everlasting, a happiness that is authentic and eternal, but
it is a way which differs from the beaten path of
cultural attitudes and values. And since the way of the
world is concerned with the things of this world, this
choice concerns those areas of behavior that are dealt
with in the commandments that govern our response
to created reality: that is, the commandments which
deal with our stance toward violence and power
("You shall not kill"); toward sex and pleasure ("You
shall not commit adultery, covet your neighbor's
wife"); toward wealth and poverty ("You shall not
steal or covet your neighbor's goods"); toward self-
respect and honesty ("You shall not bear false
witness"). When we pray "Lead us not into temptation, but deliver us from evil," our daily experience
of God's answer to this prayer is found in the ability
we experience through grace to resist the false allurements of life in this world and to remain united to
God in faith, hope and love.

In a sense, the petition "Hallowed be thy name!"
says it all. To know God's name is to know God. It
is to be in personal relationship with Him. To desire
that His name be hallowed is to surrender our whole

being to Him in praise, reverence and service. And this is what the grace of Jesus Christ is all about.[4]

FOOTNOTES

[1] See WHY JESUS?, Introduction and chapter one, pp. 8-11, for an explanation of the connection between name, person and relationship in Scripture. See also, for example, Isaiah 62:2-5; Hosea chapters 1-3; Genesis 17:5, 15; Matthew 16:18; Acts 13:2,9.

[2] See Raymond E. Brown, S.S., NEW TESTAMENT ESSAYS, "The Pater Noster as an Eschatological Prayer" (Doubleday Image Books, 1966).

[3] Loc. cit., pp. 305-307.

[4] See Appendix II, p. 191, for a method for praying over the words of the Our Father.

CHAPTER TEN: PRAY "FATHER...KINGDOM...COME!"
— *Matthew* 6:9-15

Summary:

1. The commandment "You shall not take the name of the LORD, your God, in vain" was given to teach reverence for the transcendent majesty of God. When Jesus teaches us to pray "Our Father . . . hallowed be thy name" He is teaching us intimacy and a family relationship with God. This is an implicit revelation of grace.
2. We are able to call God "Father" with the familiarity of sons because through baptism we became one with Christ by incorporation into His Body. We are *"filii in Filio,"* "sons in the Son." We are truly one with Christ, truly identified with Him as sharers in His own life. Therefore we are sons of the Father by the very fact that He is and we exist "in Him."
3. When we pray, "Hallowed be thy name," this is not just the expression of a human desire. It is a cry of wonder, praise and love which proceeds from that mystical knowledge of God which we have through union with the Son and the Spirit dwelling within us and seeing God as He is. It is already the same exclamation as that of the blessed in Heaven who cry out day and night before His throne, "Holy, holy, holy . . . !" It is the prayer of those who know God's "name" by grace. It presupposes a union of mind with God.
4. The petitions "Thy kingdom come!" and "Thy will be done . . . " express a union of will with God. They imply union with Christ in desire and dedication to His mission,

which is to bring all things in heaven and on earth together into one under His headship.

5. The rest of the petitions in the Lord's prayer put the accent on hope. This is true of the whole prayer, which is a looking forward in faith, hope and desire toward the "end time", the final victory of Christ and reunion of all creation in love around the wedding feast of the Lamb.

Questions for prayer and discussion:

1. What difference is there in the meaning God's "name" has for us in the Old Testament and in the New? What feelings are aroused in me when I say the name "God"? When I say the name "Father"? Is my relationship with God based more on awe and reverence for His transcendent majesty ("fear of the Lord"), or on a sense of family closeness and intimacy?

2. Have I in any way experienced within myself an understanding of God, of His relationship with me, which seems to come more from within me than from anything I have heard or learned from outside? When I just breathe forth prayerfully the word "God!" or "Father!" can I feel a depth of wonder, of intimacy, of love which I have no words for? Just a desire for something, for someone I know to be the answer to all my heart's longing and more desirable than I can explain?

3. Have I really embraced the desires of Christ's heart as my own, especially His desire to bring all things in heaven and on earth together into unity under His headship? What does "Thy Kingdom come!" mean to me? What in particular am I longing for when I pray "Thy will be done!"? Or is it anything particular?

4. How do I experience the Our Father as a prayer of hope? Does it give me comfort to look forward with faith to the final victory of Christ, to know that it will be accomplished? Why is this prayer addressed to the Father? Do I feel different addressing these petitions to the Father instead of to the Son or Spirit? In what way? Why is this?

CHAPTER ELEVEN

TRUST AND BE WHOLE
Fear is a Fragmentation

God has no parts. And for that reason He is unable to act with only part of His being. So when God loves, He loves with His whole heart and soul, without reserve. This is the way Jesus teaches us to love.

The first and greatest commandment, both in the Old Testament and in the New, is simply: "Hear, O Israel: The LORD is our God, the LORD alone! Therefore you shall love the LORD, your God, with all your heart, and with all your soul, and with all your strength" (*Deuteronomy* 6:4-5; see *Matthew* 22:37-40).

This is the first commandment of the Exodus list (I, the LORD, am your God . . . you shall not have other gods besides me"), and it is the last commandment Jesus comments on in the Sermon on the Mount. It brings His teaching on the law to its climax. In the teaching of Jesus, however, undivided love for God depends on absolute trust.

When God first taught this commandment through Moses, the emphasis was on acknowledging the transcendence — the differentness — of God. God is not one among many gods; not even the best and highest of the gods. God is unique. He is on an entirely different level of existence from all created things. His goodness does not enter into the scale of the created goodness we experience: it is beyond all experience, all imagining, all words. No attempt to express the goodness and reality of God can even come close. To emphasize this point, God forbade the Jews to make any image at all, whether painted or sculptured, which would pretend to represent Him (see *Exodus* 20:4-5; *Deuteronomy* 4:15-19 and 27:5,14). God reserved to Himself alone the right to determine how He would be represented in visible form. And the image God gave us was man himself — brought to perfection in Jesus Christ (see *Genesis* 1:26; *Colossians* 1:15).

A second emphasis in Moses, and the practical conclusion of his teaching, was that the Jews should show their acknowledgment of God as the one and only true God by obeying all of His commands and precepts. This is what their uprightness, their fidelity to the Covenant would consist in: "Our justice before the LORD, our God, is to consist in carefully observing all these commandments he has enjoined on us" (see *Deuteronomy* 6:1-25).

This is the justice, and the idea of religion or holiness, that people normally grow up with. To be religious, to be holy, means to keep the law, to stay within moral bounds, not to do anything wrong. The very wording of the Ten Commandments suggests this: "You shall not . . . you shall not . . . "

This understanding of religion is not so much false as it is inadequate. It belongs to the childhood stage of our religious development. As St. Paul puts it, the commandments and the religious laws which explained them were our teacher, our childhood tutor, to whose charge we were entrusted until we had grown enough to learn as adults do.

> Before faith came we were under the constraint of the law, locked in until the faith that was coming should be revealed. In other words, the law was our monitor until Christ came to bring about our justification through faith. But now that the faith is here, we are no longer in the monitor's charge. Each one of you is a son of God because of your faith in Christ Jesus.
>
> (*Galatians* 3:23-26)

St. Paul is not saying that the Ten Commandments no longer apply! (He is saying, however, that the cultural prescriptions of the Jewish law do not apply, and that the Gentile converts of his day should not be forced to obey them). What Paul is saying here is that it is not enough to be law-observers; we must be disciples (see chapter two of this book, above). And a disciple is one who seeks to "acquire a fresh, spiritual way of thinking" (*Ephesians* 4:23), to put on the "mind of Christ" (see *Romans* 12:2; 1 *Corinthians* 2:1-16). This mind of Christ — or better, this sharing in Christ's own personal, living act of knowing — is what we mean by the gift of faith.

When Jesus takes up the commandment to love the Lord, our God, with our whole heart, soul, and strength, the undivided love He teaches depends on trust: "No man can serve two masters," Jesus says. "He will either hate one and love the other or be attentive to one and despise the other. You cannot give yourself to God and money" (*Matthew* 6:24).

And therefore, He continues, "do not worry about your livelihood, what you are to eat or drink or use for clothing . . . Your heavenly Father knows all that you need."

The conclusion of Jesus' teaching here is that holiness consists in undivided love, and the only way to love God like this is to give up every earthly fear. This calls for absolute trust. For the Christian, holiness will not consist in carefully observing all of God's commandments. It is rather that we should give ourselves with our whole strength to accepting the reign of God in our hearts, surrendering to His indwelling presence, to the life and light of His Spirit by which we are called to live. We have become one with God, sharers in His life, able to act on the level of God Himself because we participate in God's own act of knowing, choosing, loving. We are members of Christ, "sons in the Son", and our life now is to let Christ live and act in us (see *Galatians* 2:20; 2 *Corinthians* 4:11-13). The God Jesus teaches us to love is our Father. He has made us one with Himself by grace. And therefore what Jesus urges us to do is "Seek first his kingship over you, his way of holiness" (*Matthew* 6:33). This is what it means to love the Lord.

It is one thing to love God as God: another thing to love Him as our Father. If God is just God, the emphasis in our relationship with Him will be on obedience and respectful fear. And God will ask nothing more of us than that we should be good human beings, living in a way appropriate to our nature as rational animals.

But if God is our Father, then the emphasis in our relationship with Him must be on trust. If God is our Father, then what He will expect of us is that we should live and act as His sons — not just as rational animals, but as sharers in the nature and life of God Himself. And only through trust in God can we do this. The power to do it must come from Him. It is utterly beyond our natural ability.

Then our holiness will consist in total surrender to the life of God; to the mission of Christ our Head; to the Spirit who lives and acts within us; to all the motions of grace. This is what it means to seek first His kingship, His reign over us. But surrender is impossible without trust.

This is the theme of Jesus' teaching in the Sermon on the Mount as He takes up, transforms, and gives back to us the Ten Commandments on the level of His new law of grace. We must live now, no longer as human beings only, but as sons and daughters of God, "In a word, you must be made perfect as your heavenly Father is perfect" (*Matthew* 5:48).

The greatest obstacle we face on this level is fear (see *Mark* 4:40; 5:15-17; 33-36). When we think of total surrender to God we are frightened both by the opposition we expect from others and by the resistance we experience within ourselves. The very prospect of a way of living so far beyond our nature causes us to feel both fear and desire. This is the way we are affected by great speed, great height, greath depth. Our fear of following Christ begins however, with an undramatically ground level anticipation of hardship to be endured in this world.

The way of God, as we pointed out in the last chapter, is simply not in harmony with the way of the "world." The law of Christ does not impress unbelievers and pagans the way Moses said the law of the Old Testament would:

Therefore I teach you the statues and decrees as the LORD, my God, has commanded me, that you may observe them in the land you are entering to occupy. Observe them carefully, for thus will you give evidence of your wisdom and intelligence to the nations, who will hear of all these statutes and say, "This great nation is truly a wise and intelligent people".

(*Deuteronomy* 4:5-6)

On the contrary, St. Paul says that Christ's teaching is "complete absurdity" to those who do not accept it with the grace of faith. It appears to the wise of this world to be foolishness, and those who follow it are made "fools on Christ's account" (see 2 *Corinthians* 1:18 ff. and 4:9-13).

As a result, those who follow the way of Christ must be willing to risk the loss of everything else: money, friends, family approval, social acceptance, even life itself (see *Matthew* 8:19-22; 10:16 ff.; 16:24-27; *Luke* 12:1 ff.; 14:26-30). Those who are afraid; those whose hearts are divided between love for Christ and love for this world; between desire for the gift of new life which Jesus gives to His followers and desire for the favors which this world bestows on those who are its own, cannot enter fully into this union with God which is offered.

An undivided heart: this is the climax of Jesus' teaching in the Sermon on the Mount: "No man can serve two masters . . . Seek first the kingship of God over you . . . Do not lay up for yourselves an earthly treasure . . . Do not worry about your livelihood, what you are to eat or drink or use for clothing . . . Stop worrying over questions like these" (see *Matthew* 6:19-34). But this teaching is combined with some of Jesus' most gentle sayings about the Father: "Look at the birds in the sky. They do not sow or reap, they gather nothing into barns; yet your heavenly Father feeds them. Are not you more important than they? . . . Stop worrying, then . . . Your heavenly Father knows all that you need."

In other places Jesus holds up before us the promise of God's fatherly love and providence at the same time that He prepares us for persecution (see *Matthew* 10:16-42 and especially *Luke* 12:2-34, which combines the persecution passage of *Matthew* 10:26-33 with the providence passage of *Matthew* 6:26-34. See also *John* 14-16). In the Sermon on the Mount, however, the encouragement to trust in God and fear nothing is combined with Jesus' exhortation to simply love God with an undivided heart. In order to keep the great commandment: "You shall love the Lord, your God, with all your heart, and with all your soul, and with all your strength," what we have most need of is absolute trust in the saving love of God our Father. Fear is a fragmentation. The exhortation of Jesus is that we should trust in God and be whole.

CHAPTER ELEVEN: TRUST AND BE WHOLE —
Matthew 6:19-34

Summary:

1. In the Law that was given on Mount Sinai, the first commandment was "I, the LORD, am your God . . . you shall not have other gods besides me." This became the Great Commandment: "Hear, O Israel: The LORD is our God, the LORD alone! Therefore you shall love the LORD, your God, with all your heart, with all your soul, and with all your strength." This is a summons to undivided love and loyalty toward God. The emphasis, however, is on God's transcendence, His uniqueness, His differentness from all creation. The emphasis of this commandment is on awe and reverence, and on a love which takes the form of total, absolute obedience to the will and to the law of God.

2. In Jesus' Sermon on the Mount the Great Commandment is still the same, but its meaning is transformed. Jesus calls us, not just to give to the transcendent God with all our human strength the love and loyalty that is His due, but to surrender our whole selves to living and loving on God's own level. This is a surrender to become one with God, sharers in His own life and action. It is a way of "losing" ourselves on the human level (without detracting from the human at all) in order to "find" ourselves in union with God. It is total surrender and total gift for the sake of total union.

3. This is to give up control of ourselves in a very profound and radical way. We keep our free wills. There can be no graced act on our part unless we freely and deliberately cooperate in it. But in graced action we use our freedom to let God act in us, to live according to His own mind and heart, acting by His power, His love. This is different from simply using our intellects and wills, our human powers, to observe the laws of behavior proper to human beings. Graced living is living in total surrender to God's inspirations and movements, in total dependence on His enabling love. That is why it calls for absolute trust.

4. Once we decide to surrender to God in grace, our greatest obstacle is fear. We fear the opposition of men, the loss of material goods and security, the loss of life itself. But our most profound fear — which is perhaps not clearly recognized — is simply the fear of "losing ourselves" in God, of surrendering to the unknown of His mind, His desires, His unpredictable life in us, our unfathomable future in Him. For this reason Jesus' teaching on the Great Commandment is a teaching that calls us to absolute trust in the Father.

Questions for prayer and discussion:

1. What is the difference between loving and obeying the Lord with my whole human strength, because of His greatness, and surrendering myself to live and love on His level, by the power of His life poured out within me? Have I experienced this difference in any concrete ways in my life? How?

2. In what ways do I find fear an obstacle to total surrender to Jesus Christ? To the teaching of His Gospel? How would undivided loyalty to Jesus bring me into conflict with the people in my life? With my family? My friends? My business associates? Would I risk the loss of any material possessions if I lived the Gospel with my whole heart? How?

3. What assurance has God given me in my heart — in my prayer, or through my experience of His dealings with me — that He will take care of me if I live unhesitatingly for Him? Are there times when I have had the courage to do this? Times when I haven't? How do I feel about those times now?

4. In what concrete and realistic ways — consistent with my situation in life — can I choose "not to lay up for myself an earthly treasure?" Do I in any sense serve "two masters?" Does this affect in any way the "light" I live and choose by? How? What practical application can I make of Christ's words here to my own life?

CHAPTER TWELVE

THE LIGHT OF
FAITH-COMMUNITY: DISCERNMENT
Your Depth Is the Light You Judge By

The Old Law — the law of the Ten Commandments, of the Scriptural books Exodus, Leviticus, Numbers and Deuteronomy — was very much a law to help human beings live together peacefully in community. The community was characterized by its fidelity to God, of course. But this fidelity to God, and to the laws God established, would keep the people living in peace and harmony with one another. And as we have seen (chapter three above) the laws God laid down for His people were essentially directives for living in this world according to human nature rationally understood.

By contrast, the Sermon on the Mount is essentially an instruction on how to live as sharers in the nature of God. The New Law of Jesus is the law God lives by. It is not the law appropriate to creatures, even to rational creatures, but to the unique, divine being of God Himself. Although Jesus' version of the Commandments does teach us to relate to one another in community, its focus is not there. Its focus is on relationship with God. The law of Jesus that we have seen so far directly addresses interior attitudes more than it does external behavior. The union it focuses on is union of mind and heart and will with God; this, rather than relationship within the community of believers as such, is the immediate object of the passages we have seen.[1]

In chapter seven, however, the Sermon on the Mount takes up directly the life and mutual interaction of the believing community as such.

It would be logical to expect that, just as the new law of Jesus for individuals is a law for living like God, so the new law for Christian communities should be a law for living in heaven. People who think and act like God should make life a heaven on earth for one another.

This is logical, but it isn't true to life; it leaves out an element of reality, which is the fact of sin. We who are called to live by the life of God are all sinners, and we remain sinners until the day we die. The real challenge of Christian community is to keep striving to live by the standards of God in loving union with other people who are also striving, but who are not succeeding at it any better than we are. The truth of the matter is, we experience the communion of saints only in a community of sinners.

And so Christ's law for Christian community is very realistic. It takes for granted that the community will always have to struggle against the divisive elements of judgmentalism, mutual disagreement, selfishness, laxity and illusion. Our Lord acknowledges the threat of these realities and gives His answer to the problems they present.

Do not judge . . .

The greatest threat to unity and love in any group is pride. This is because the essence of pride is to make one's own self the criterion of right and wrong, truth and falsity. Thus the only way to be united with a person who is proud is to make him or her one's God.

When a young man called Jesus "good Teacher . . . " Jesus replied, "Why do you call me good? No one is good but God alone" (*Mark* 10:17-18; cf. *Matthew* 19:17). Only God is good absolutely. It is only God whose behavior can be taken as the very criterion itself of truth and falsity. In the absolute sense, only God truly is anything, because God alone is absolute Truth, Being, Goodness. All creatures are only images and approximations of what exists perfectly in God. To this extent Plato was onto something true when he explained reality in terms of shadow-images dancing on the wall of a cave.[2]

When Jesus challenged the young man for calling Him "Good Teacher", He was not really repudiating the title. Jesus did, as a matter of fact, claim to be the one and only Teacher in the absolute sense. "Avoid being called teachers," He told His disciples. "Only one is your teacher, the Messiah" (*Matthew* 23:10). Later He said of Himself, "I *am* the way, and the truth, and the life" (*John* 14:6). So in this incident, what Jesus is doing is inciting the young man to think, and to decide ahead of time whether he will accept the answer Jesus is going to give to his question as an answer that comes from God. Jesus doesn't debate as a fellow-searcher discussing things with equals; He teaches as one who knows (see *John* 3:1-21). It is only by putting our faith in Him absolutely ahead of time that we can accept as true and good the teachings of Jesus which go beyond the natural level of our understanding and ideals.

Here we have the answer to pride, and the only authentic source of union of mind between believers. To be a disciple of Jesus is to be surrendered to a truth that comes from God — a truth beyond human discovering, a truth beyond human comprehension, that no human being can ever master as his own so as to teach it with the authority of a master (see *Matthew* 23:8,10). This is the essence of humility: to know that one is *not* the criterion: that one's own opinions are not the criterion of truth, one's own desires and behavior are not the criterion of goodness; that one's own way of experiencing and reacting is not the criterion of reality.

And this is the condition for living in Christian community.

A community of believers is a community of people submitted to a truth that is constantly coming from above — or from the Spirit of God speaking within the heart of each one. This is not to say that truth once revealed and formulated can be denied; that doctrine can develop into a contradiction of itself, or that there is no such thing as timeless, unchanging truth. It simply means that in the life of the believing community, God is always speaking, always enlightening, always showing people in new, insightful ways how the truth already accepted is to be understood and applied to life. The truth of Christianity is a dynamic, not a static truth. It is a living word. And for this very reason those who are united in their acceptance of Christ's teaching are always in danger of becoming disunited in their understanding and application of it. Where the word of God is truly active and alive, truly living in our hearts, that word will move individuals to take courses of action which are new and prophetic. And until the community can judge what is new and be reunited in acceptance of it, there is danger of division.

The response Jesus makes to this danger in the Sermon on the Mount is, "Do not judge" (see *Matthew* 7:1-5). In a Christian community people must be very careful not to make judgments about the faith-responses of other people. The reason is that when people are responding to God, their actions cannot be judged by common sense alone. They can only be judged by someone who knows what it is to be spoken to by God, and what the signs are of authentic response to grace. Ultimately, the judgment of others' prophetic movements belongs to the community alone, not to any individual in it, unless he can speak with the authority of the community itself (see *Matthew* 18:17; 1 *Corinthians* 14:29).

When Jesus says, "If you want to avoid judgment, stop passing judgment; your verdict on others will be the verdict passed on you" (*Matthew* 7:1-2), we automatically assume He is speaking here about the judgment we pass on others' sins. And this is a legitimate interpretation: it is an axiom in Christianity that while we know certain actions are sinful in themselves, and objectively wrong, we can never judge the subjective guilt of another person's heart. We can condemn the sin but not the sinner. We just never know how clearly another person perceives that what he or she is doing is wrong, or how freely and deliberately a person is choosing to engage in a particular kind of behavior. And therefore we can say about our brother's action that it is folly, but we can never say to our brother, "You are a fool" (see *Matthew* 5:22).

There is another way to interpret this passage, however. In a Christian community the greatest source of division is not found in the obvious sins people commit. Obvious sins are matter for forgiveness, not for disagreement. The source of disunity that we might call most authentically Christian, most characteristic of truly Christian communities, is disagreement over what is the better, the more appropriately Christian thing to do.

The hardest fights in most Christian communities are over matters which hardly touch on faith or morals. What should be the wording of the prayers? the language used in the liturgy? the form of the worship service? How should communion be distributed? Who should be allowed to preach? to be ordained? What decorations should be seen, what music heard, what dress is appropriate in church?

And then there are the prophets. St. Francis of Assisi was a scandal to the Catholics of his day, and John Wesley to the Angelicans of his, not because of their doctrine, but because of their devotion. When God moves someone to live the Gospel more fervently, more authentically, in a way that is more challenging to the spirit of the times, the first effect of this movement is usually a disturbance in the Church. When this happens, the word of Jesus to every individual is a warning not to judge.

We cannot judge, but we must discern! Jesus will say just a few paragraphs later, "Be on your guard against false prophets . . . " (*Matthew* 7:15). How do we reconcile these two directives?

The key to the warning not to judge is this: "Your verdict on others will be the verdict passed on you.

The measure with which you measure will be used to measure you" (*Matthew* 7:2). If we measure our brother's behavior by a standard of common sense alone, we pass verdict on ourselves for not being spiritual men and women. If we react against our brother's behavior because it threatens our own mediocrity, apathy or fear, we reveal in that action what we are and what the level is of our spiritual lives. It is our condemnation of others that condemns us.

The most explicit and developed teaching in the New Testament on this point is found in St. Paul's first letter to the Corinthians, chapters two to six. In these chapters Paul is basically telling the Corinthians that they are not spiritually mature enough to judge matters according to the Spirit of God. "Brothers, the trouble was that I could not talk to you as spiritual men but only as men of flesh, as infants in Christ. I fed you with milk, and did not give you solid food because you were not ready for it. You are not ready for it even now, being still very much in a natural condition" (1 *Corinthians* 3:1-2). How can the Corinthians see to judge what is and is not a movement of the Holy Spirit when their conduct shows that they are still on the human level, seeing things through the eyes of unenlightened reason, and not with the vision of faith and love? "For as long as there are jealousy and quarrels among you, are you not of the flesh? And is not your behavior that of ordinary men? . . . Is it not clear that you are still at the human level?" (1 *Corinthians* 3:3-4). St. Paul could have quoted the Sermon on the Mount here: "How can you say to your brother, 'Let me take that speck out of your eye,' while all the time the plank remains in your own?" (*Matthew* 7:4). How can you presume to judge whether another is or is not responding to the Holy

Spirit when you yourself are obviously not living in response to the Spirit? Those whose thinking rises no higher than the plane of ordinary, human common sense are simply not able to judge the worth of what is going on in the Church. As St. Paul insists:

> The natural man does not accept what is taught by the Spirit of God. For him, that is absurdity. He cannot come to know such teaching because it must be appraised in a spiritual way. The spiritual man, on the other hand, can appraise everything, though He himself can be appraised by no one. For, "Who has known the mind of the Lord so as to instruct him?" But we have the mind of Christ.
> (1 *Corinthians* 2:14-16)

The early Church, being then as now a human as well as a divine organization, was torn by factions and human disagreements. There were passion and sin on both sides of every issue that divided the believers into opposing camps. (For some samples, see *Galatians,* chapter two and *Acts* 15:27-39). But when the community set itself to come together into unity and to discern how the Spirit of God was moving them, they made their decisions according to three norms: reason, spiritual experience, and Scripture.

The first Council of the Church, the Council of Jerusalem, in which the most threatening and divisive question of apostolic times was settled, is an example of this. It began with an argument by Peter (*Acts* 15:6-11) in which he drew rational conclusions from his own spiritual experience (cf. *Acts,* chapters 10-11). Paul and Barnabas then described their experiences of God working wonders through them among the Gentiles (*Acts* 15:12). Finally the apostle James stood up and showed how everything that was being said was in accordance with Scripture (*Acts* 5:13-19). And he suggested a practical course of action which was new, without precedent in the history of God's people, and which was not a conclusion from Scripture but simply a reasonable compromise capable of uniting both sides (*Acts* 15:20-29).

Of the four rules that came out of that Council (see *Acts* 15:29), three (the dietary restrictions) have no relevance or force of law today. The Council's response to the situation the Church faced at that time was an act of government that was both human and divine: a course of action prescribed for the Church in that day which came out of human reasoning, divine inspiration and practical politics. It was a decision which was partly temporary — the particular rules it contained did not last any longer than the situation which called for them — and at the same time permanent: it settled for all time the question of whether Christianity was essentially a Jewish religion, inseparably wedded to observance of the Mosaic law. It was a decision which combined the temporary and the permanent, the practical considerations of time, place and culture with the absolute demands of orthodox doctrine and response to the Holy Spirit. As such it was a truly Christian decision: that is, a combination of the human and the divine. And it was a decision not to be judged by the spiritually immature, but only by those who, like St. Paul, had done what was necessary in response to grace to take on the "mind of Christ." It called for acceptance and obedience in faith.

In the Sermon on the Mount, when Jesus teaches us not to be judgmental in our reactions to the behavior of other people, He is telling us something about the level of decision-making that should be maintained in the Christian community. A community of believers cannot — should not — find sufficient guidance for their lives — either as individuals or as a community — in the law alone. As disciples of Jesus, Christians must strive to base their decisions and their conduct on the principles taught by Jesus, and principles are not the same as laws (see above, chapter two). Laws are the conclusion of a thought process; principles are the beginning of one. For this reason wherever discipleship is authentic, the teachings of Jesus continuously give birth to creative insights, spiritual initiatives, new ways of appreciating and living the Gospel. This calls for discernment. The believing community must constantly observe, listen, discuss, pray over and discern what the Spirit of God is saying in its midst. The community must remain open and take the responsibility of prayerfully judging the initiatives and suggestions which arise from its members. For this task, those who engage in it must be disciples. They must be students of the Spirit, people of spiritual depth, who are trying, to the best of their ability, to "remove the plank" from their own eye first (see *Matthew* 7:5) so that they might be able to see and judge with the clear-eyed vision of faith.

To judge prayerfully and respectfully, together with others in community — which is to discern — this is not the judgment Christ condemns in His Sermon on the Mount. The judgmentalism He condemns is that of pride, which makes one's own self, one's own way, one's own prejudices the criterion of truth and falsity, of right and wrong. (Or which makes the law alone the criterion, which is Phariseeism). Those who discern take, or try to take, the action of the Spirit in their midst as their criterion, together with the Scriptures and calm reasoning in dialogue with others. This is a process which begins and ends with a humble awareness of how large is the plank in one's own eye, and which calls for soul-searching efforts to remove it.

Jesus follows His warning against judgmentalism with another teaching which sounds about as judgmental as one can get! "Do not give what is holy to dogs or toss your pearls before swine. They will trample them under foot, at best, and perhaps even tear you to shreds" (*Matthew* 7:6).

A theology professor once said, when his class was preparing to leave after a particularly heated discussion: "Wait, gentlemen: I have a few more pearls to cast!" That was judgmental! But the thrust of Jesus' remarks is love: He is calling for a sensitivity in community which respects where other people are in their understanding and ability to hear. His teaching here is essentially the same as the answer He gave to John the Baptizer's disciples, when He pointed out that no one sews a piece of new cloth on an old coat or pours new wine into old wineskins (*Matthew* 11:16-17). To give to anybody something he is not yet ready to hear is destructive. And those who feel threatened by teaching that is beyond their comprehension or by ideals which exceed their generosity are liable to take defense measures. Typically they will jump all over the truth they are being taught and at the same time attack the reputation of the teacher. They will try to rip his credibility apart. Anyone who has ever tried to argue ideals with a group which doesn't want to accept them knows that people who are threatened never play fair! They bypass the arguments like a mad bull ignoring the cape and go straight for the living flesh!

The exhortation of Jesus here is to avoid setting up situations which are bound to lead to nothing but disunion and hostility. Sometimes, of course, this cannot be avoided. Then the prophet must simply stand up and let himself be stoned. But it is part of the love and respect which we owe to others in community not to say things to people which they are not yet able to hear. God respects the human pace at which people grow into new attitudes and values; and so, out of reverence for other persons' freedom, should we.

Jesus' instructions here — do not judge, and do not cast pearls before swine — call for a double respect within the Christian community: respect for the divine level on which the community is called to judge and to act; and respect for the human pace at which people normally change. They remind us that a community of believers is a divine and human reality; a society of men and women who share in the nature of God, but who are nonetheless human for that. And this will be the theme of everything we say about Christian community: that the Church wherever it is found, in every assembly of believers, whether they gather at home as a family, in small groups for mutual assistance, or in churches to worship together, is always a community of people striving together to live on the level of God and of man simultaneously. This is what it means to live by grace, to embody the inspirations of the Spirit in actions of flesh and blood. And for that reason, those who would judge the behavior of others, or the decisions of the community as such, must be sure of the Spirit within them.

FOOTNOTES

[1] This is the author's opinion, at least. The passages are open to other interpretation. An exception to this explanation could be *Matthew* 5:23-24.

All that Jesus teaches about relationship with the neighbor has an impact on the life of the believing community, of course. But as we have seen, Jesus' teaching on these commandments begins and ends with the fact, which is also the good news, of each individual's transforming union with God in grace. That, I believe, is the real focus.

[2] See *The Republic,* Book VII.

CHAPTER TWELVE: THE LIGHT OF FAITH-COMMUNITY: DISCERNMENT — *Matthew* 7:1-6

Summary:

1. In chapter seven the Sermon on the Mount takes up the guidelines that should govern the life and interaction of the Christian community. The problem of relationship in the Church is that people are called and must try to live on the level of God while in their human reality they remain subject to all sorts of false assumptions, weaknesses and woundedness. The communion of saints can only be experienced within a community of sinners. All relationships within the Church must be based on recognition and acceptance of this reality.

2. The first thing Jesus warns us against is presuming to judge others' inspirations and responses to grace. The greatest threat to unity in any group is pride, because the essence of pride is to make one's own self the criterion of truth and falsity, of good and evil. Only God is the criterion, and unity within the Christian community depends on being able to use God as the criterion of all judgments and decisions. In a Christian community any other criterion is divisive by nature.

3. The truth Christians live by is dynamic, not static. The truth Jesus taught is timeless and unchanging, and we can arrive at certain formulations or expressions of His truth that are valid for all times. But the Christian community is always growing in her understanding of Christ's teaching, and

always receiving new, prophetic insights on how to apply it to the challenges of modern life. Whenever this happens there is danger of division until the community can judge what is new and be reunited in acceptance of it. This judgment must be made by the community itself, and no individual should presume to judge another unless he has the authority to speak for the community as such.

4. Those who are obliged to judge, or to participate in the judgment of another's prophetic stance, must be people who know what it is to be spoken to by God, and what the signs are of authentic response to grace. They must be prudent and spiritual men. The standard by which they judge will be the judgment on their own spiritual depth. The standard by which a community makes its own decisions and passes judgment on the decisions of others will be judgment of its spiritual depth as a community.

5. The disciples of Jesus cannot base their lives or their decisions as a community on law alone. The light which a faith-community lives by is discernment of the action of the Holy Spirit in its midst. Knowledge of and adherence to sound doctrine is an element of this discernment. So is commonsense reasoning about the reality of the practical situation. A third element is recognition of the spiritual experiences, inspirations, etc. of the members or of the community as a whole. These three elements are found in the first Council of the Church, recorded in *Acts,* chapter 15.

Questions for prayer and discussion:

1. Have I ever found the human weaknesses, prejudices, etc. in the Christian community (in its members or in its leaders) to be a real obstacle to my belief in the community itself? To my trust that God can act and is acting through it? To my love and loyalty toward the community? What role does acceptance of sin and sinners play in my relationship with the Christian community?

2. Do I understand pride as the act of making oneself the criterion of truth and falsehood, good and evil? How does this differ from conceit, or just having an exaggerated opinion of one's good qualities? Why does pride make unity within the community impossible? Is my own pride the source of any divisions between myself and others?

3. What examples of change or of innovation can I think of which have caused division in the Church? How were these judged or evaluated by the community? By what process or norms did I judge them? Was the result peace or division?

4. Have I ever seen a Christian community make decisions according to the three elements found in *Acts*, chapter 15? How did this come about? Have I ever made decisions myself using these three norms? Which element would I say is most frequently missing in my own decisions? In those of the community? Why is this?

CHAPTER THIRTEEN

THE POWER OF
FAITH-COMMUNITY: PRAYER
I Am the Beginning and the End

The Spirit of God gives life to a Christian community the way sap gives life to a tree. A tree without sap is dead wood: it still looks like a tree, has the shape of a tree, and is even able to hold itself together and stand upright for years as if it were a tree. But its wood is dry, its life is gone, and it cannot produce any living thing, neither leaf or fruit. Basically, it "clutters up the ground" (see *Luke* 13:7).

The same is true of a Christian community which does not live by the Spirit of God. It may look like a church community; it may even hold together for years, taking up space. But essentially it is dead wood, and its members will begin dropping off one by one until the whole community either falls apart or decides to listen to the voice of God calling it to rise from the dead (see *Ezekiel* 37:1-14).

To live by the Spirit is to stay in touch with the Spirit, paying attention to His inspirations, following His movements, relying on His power. A community

which lives by the Spirit makes its decisions and
judgments, not according to common sense and
natural reasoning alone, but by a prayerful discernment of what the Spirit of God is doing in its midst.
This was the point of our last chapter.

The next thing Jesus says in the Sermon on the
Mount is a further teaching on Christian community;
it tells us where the power comes from: "Ask, and you
will receive. Seek, and you will find. Knock, and it
will be opened to you," (*Matthew* 7:7).

To remain authentic, a Christian community has
to maintain itself in a constant, conscious awareness
of dependence on God. The concrete expression of
this is prayer.

The spirit of Jesus' teaching here is in direct
contradiction to the saying we frequently hear, "Well,
there is nothing we can do now but pray." For a
Christian community prayer is the first thing to do,
not the last. The spirit of the Gospel is not that we
should first do all in our power to resolve our
problems by human means, and when all else fails,
turn to God. To live in this mentality is to totally
misunderstand the reality of Christian existence,
which is a union of God and man in grace.

Christians do not see two ways of accomplishing
things: by man's power or by God's. They see only
one way to do anything authentically as Christians,
and that is by letting God's power act through and
within human efforts. An authentically Christian act
is like the actions of Jesus Himself: it is at one and the
same time both human and divine. The more fully
human and fully divine it is, the more it approaches
the perfection of graced Christian activity. This
means that the ideal of Christian activity is to use
all of one's human powers and faculties to the utmost,

while at the same time acting entirely by the inspiration and power of Christ.

Christians are the Body of Christ. They only act authentically as Christians when they act as members of Christ; that is, when Christ is acting in them. And Jesus acts in His members through the unifying principle of His Body, which is the Spirit. Through the inspirations of His Spirit Jesus enlightens, excites, strengthens and guides each individual member and the Christian community as a whole. To act as a member of the Body of Christ, then, is to move in response to the head, who is Jesus (see *Ephesians* 1:22; 4:15-16; 5:23). And the life-giving link between the head and the members is the Spirit. It is clear, then, that the beginning, middle and end of every Christian act should be an effort to keep in contact with Christ through His Spirit. This is prayer.

Prayer has many different forms, and the word can mean many different things, depending on what one is seeking in prayer. Outlines of two different methods for learning how to pray are appended to this book, and I have explained another method elsewhere, which I would call the prayer of "encounter with Jesus," or simply the "prayer of discipleship."[1] But in this passage of the Sermon on the Mount Jesus is speaking of another kind of prayer, which is the prayer of *petition,* or (when our petitions are for the sake of others) *intercessory prayer.*

Petitionary prayer is just asking. The *Our Father* is essentially a prayer of petition, although the petitions it is composed of, having been taught to us by Christ Himself, are also guidelines to meditate on. They instruct the heart. In this passage, however (*Matthew* 7:7-11), Jesus is not teaching us a formula for prayer but a spirit. It is a spirit of dependence and of filial trust. And it is nourished by asking.

You, He says, who are sinners, know how to give good things to your children. "Would one of you hand his son a stone when he asks for a loaf, or a poisonous snake when he asks for a fish?" (*Matthew* 7:9-11). Well, if you understand what grace (the favor of union with God) really is, you will know that you are sons of your Father in heaven. You will trust Him and depend on Him for everything you need, the way children place trust in their fathers.

The Christian community lives in a spirit of dependence which looks to the Father to provide for all its needs. This is not, however, the kind of dependence that every creature has on God. It is more than that. What the Christian community is all about is living the life of God. We are not just creatures but "sons in the Son." We have been made divine in Christ. The life we live now is not our own, but Christ lives in us (see *Galatians* 2:20; 2 *Corinthians* 13:3-5; 1 *Thessalonians* 2:11-12). We are called to live now, not on our natural level but on His (see *Colossians* 3:1 ff. and 1 *Corinthians* 15:48). To live as Christ involves taking on the attitudes and values of Christ, the priorities of His kingdom, loving one another as He Himself has loved us. This is manifestly beyond the natural range of our intellects and wills. We not only lack the generosity to do this; we cannot even conceive of what it is. Left to our human intelligence, prudence, idealism and love, we simply can't function as Christians, because to function as Christians is to function on the level of God, which is beyond us. And therefore the teaching of Jesus here is a teaching which concerns the Christian community as such.

You, He tells us — you who are trying to live as a community of divine life on earth, you must ask constantly for light and life from your Father. If you do not, you will forget what you are and what you are called to be. You will forget what level of life your judgments and choices should be on, and you will begin to live by the commonsense prudence and values of this world. You will profess my principles in words; you will parrot the Scriptures and speak very piously about love of neighbor and God. But in your actual, day-by-day choices you will walk and think and choose by the light of this world. To guard against this, pray constantly to your Father — individually and as a community — in order to keep yourselves aware of how radically different you are called to be and how radically you depend on the action of God within you in order to be what you are called to be.

"Ask and you will receive" is not just an exhortation to trust; it is an instruction on what Christian community is supposed to be: a community called to live on the level of God Himself, unable to do anything at all on this, its authentic level, except by the power of God. The Christian community depends on prayer like an airplane depends on its wings. Prayer is what holds it up.

The constant tendency in Christian communities is for their decision-making bodies — whether they are called elders, parish councils, vestries, governing boards or whatever — to initiate, discuss, and decide policy on the basis of common sense, natural reason and prudence. Very often the people named to these decision-making bodies are chosen either because of their business acumen and professional effectiveness, or because they represent the attitudes and values of a large percentage of the congregation. As a result the decisions made are too frequently logical, reasonable, and uninspired. They are not "received" as an answer to asking, but arrived at through prudent discussion. They are human decisions with very little to suggest that they might also be divine. They are not prophetic. They are not the fruit of prayer.

What Jesus teaches here is that the Christian community, both in its decision-making and in its efforts to carry out its decisions, should live by prayer. The way to receive light on any question is to ask. The way to find God's way — the authentically Christian way — of responding to any situation is to seek a response on God's level. The way to gain entrance into the wisdom and counsel of God is to stand at the door and knock. "For the one who asks, receives. The one who seeks, finds. The one who knocks, enters" (*Matthew* 7:8). Those, on the other hand, who neither ask nor seek nor knock never discover what Christian community is.

FOOTNOTE

[1] See HIS WAY, ch. 3-4 (St. Anthony Messenger Press, 1977). More explanation is given in LIFT UP YOUR EYES TO THE MOUNTAIN, ch. 2 (Dimension Books, 1981); and WHY JESUS?, ch. 5 (Dimension Books, 1981).

CHAPTER THIRTEEN: THE POWER OF FAITH-COMMUNITY: PRAYER — *Matthew* 7:7-11

Summary:

1. The life of a Christian community comes from the Spirit of God present and working within it. To remain authentic, a Christian community must maintain itself in a constant, conscious awareness of dependence on God. One concrete expression of this dependence is prayer.

2. Christians do not see two ways of accomplishing things: by man's power or by God's. The authentically Christian way is to let God's power act in and through human efforts. To be graced, an act must be simultaneously human and divine: the action of God and man acting together as one. Prayer is a means to maintain that contact with Christ which allows us to act as one with Him.

3. In this passage Jesus is exhorting us to trust in God. He appeals to our human understanding of fatherhood to convince us that God our Father will not refuse to provide us with anything that is for our good. He urges us to ask, to seek, to knock as an expression of trust and confidence in God.

4. The Christian community's dependence on God, however, is not just the basic dependence on God that belongs to every creature. Since Christians are called to act on the level of God by grace, they depend on God's grace for every Christian decision, ideal, inspiration and desire, not to mention the strength to carry these out into action. If the Christian community only asked for God's help when its own light and strength proved insufficient, this would distort its understanding of itself. It is by praying before, during and after every action that the community remains aware of its radical dependence on God to initiate, guide, carry through and bring to a desirable conclusion everything it does.

5. Our Lord's exhortation here is not just an encouragement to pray. It is also an insistence that we should remain conscious of what we are. We are a community called to live and to act on the level of God Himself. This awareness is inseparable from a sense of radical dependence on God. It is maintained and nourished by prayer. This prayer should be, not just an individual expression, but the conscious, public expression of the community as a whole.

Questions for prayer and discussion:

1. How does prayer express dependence on God? Is it only the prayer of petition that expresses this? What other kinds of prayer show that we are aware of depending on God for light to live by? How many ways do I express my dependence on God through prayer? How often do I do this?

2. What is wrong with the expression, "There is nothing to do now but pray?" What should our attitude be? How is this attitude expressed in my own life? In the life of my Christian community?

3. Do I trust God to provide for me the way I trust (or trusted) my own father? The way I want (or would want) my children to trust in me? What makes it difficult for me to trust God like this? How would I answer this difficulty? Do I ever have the chance to simply choose to trust in God? When? How do I respond on these occasions?

4. What could I do to keep myself aware of the level I am called to live on? How can I keep my judgments, decisions and actions from staying on the plane of good, human common sense? What would help me to see, judge and act constantly on the level of grace?

5. What can I do to help my Christian community do all the things mentioned in the previous question?

CHAPTER FOURTEEN

THE VALUE YOU RESPECT
IS THE VALUE YOU PROJECT

Reverencing Grace in Others

A man of the Ngama tribe in Chad, Africa, once said about the members of a particular Christian sect in his country: "As soon as a man becomes a Christian, he begins to despise his brothers."

Unfortunately, Christian history too often bears out this accusation. The attitude taken toward the "heathen" by the Spanish conquistadores, the New England Puritans, the evangelical pioneers of the Indian wars, gives substance to the cynical ditty:

First they fell upon their knees
Then fell upon the aborigines.

In order to keep the Christian community from ever taking a stance of superiority toward any other person or group, Jesus instructed His followers: "Treat others the way you would have them treat you: this sums up the law and the prophets" (*Matthew* 7:12).

This teaching is addressed to the community as a whole. The verbs and pronouns are all in the second person plural: "You (plural) treat others as you would have them treat you." If Christians understand themselves as they should — that is, if they appreciate their own sacred dignity as sons and daughters of God, members of the Body of Christ on earth — then this teaching calls upon them to treat others who are not Christians with a respect like that which is due to God Himself (see *Ephesians* 6:5).

"Treat others the way you would have them treat you:" the teaching is clear. If Christians want to be recognized as the sacred Body of Christ on earth, as children of God and temples of the Holy Spirit, then they should give to others the same reverence and respect which they believe is due to themselves.

Christianity brought human rights into focus. The martyrs who suffered for their faith claimed a divine right to obey God rather than men (see *Acts* 4:19). Christian prophets and saints throughout the ages have insisted on the right to follow God's inspirations, even when this brought them into conflict with the attitudes and values current in their times. Unfortunately, however, Christians were not so quick to accord to non-Christians, or even to other Christians judged guilty of heresy, the same right to freedom of conscience which they claimed for themselves. In this they were not following the teaching of Jesus: "Treat others the way you would have them treat you." In modern times, most Christian bodies have come to see that the right to freedom of conscience is a two-way street: Christians must respect it in others as much as they insist that it be respected in themselves.[1]

Is it exaggerated to say that Christians should give to others the same reverence that they feel is due to themselves? After all, Christians believe that they really have been transformed and sanctified by grace, that they are true children of the Father (see *Romans* 8:16, 9:8); sharers in the divine nature of God (see 2 *Peter* 1:4); members of the Body of Jesus Christ and temples of the Holy Spirit (see *Galatians,* chapters 1 and 2; 1 *Corinthians* 6:19). Those who have not been reborn by grace are none of these things. Why, then, should Christians treat others as if they were?

One reason, of course, is that it is impossible for us to say that another person has not, in fact, been reborn by grace. There are "anonymous Christians" who, without formal initiation into any church, have been reborn by "baptism of desire."[2]

But an even stronger reason is simply the fact that Jesus told us to treat others the way we would like to be treated, and He set us the example of this Himself.

Jesus was Lord and God. He deserved to be treated as such. And so, as an example of His own commandment, He "emptied himself, and took the form of a slave." He was born in the likeness of men (see *Philippians* 2:1-11); and then, insofar as it was legitimate and possible, He treated human beings as His God.

The book of Deuteronomy said, "The LORD, your God, shall you fear; him shall you serve" (*Deuteronomy* 6:13; see also *Matthew* 4:10). So Jesus came among men, not to be served, but to serve (see *Mark* 10:45; *Luke* 22:37). He washed His disciples' feet like a servant and taught them to do the same for one another (*John* 13:1-17).

The devout have always recognized that it is the duty of believers to die for the sake of God, in order to be faithful to Him (see 2 *Maccabees* 6:24-31 and all of chapter seven). In Jesus God died for the sake of men, to be faithful to His promise to them. "Treat others the way you would have them treat you."

The more appreciation Christians have, then, for their own sacredness and transformation by grace, the more reverence and respect they should show toward others who are not Christian, or who — to all outward appearances, at least — have not been so transformed and sanctified.

This principle applies to everything that Christians consider a grace. In the measure that any group of Christians judge themselves to be blessed with the gifts of the Holy Spirit, they should show reverence for the charismatic gifts of others, whether or not they are able to recognize them. In the measure that Christians feel themselves to be enlightened by prayer, they should presume that all others with whom they deal are similarly graced with particular light from God, and they should listen to them with respect. Christians who manage to be virtuous should treat everyone else on earth with the respect due to virtuous men and women. And those who are grateful for God's compassionate forgiveness toward themselves should be equally compassionate and forgiving toward others (see *Matthew* 18:32-33). This is the rule of the Gospel: "Treat others the way you would have them treat you."

There is no simplistic naivete in this. To respect others for the lights and graces God may be giving them is not to assume blindly that others are inspired by God, or even that they are in the way of truth. It just means that we respect each person for the mysterious and unknown way in which God deals with each one. And while holding to the truth of what God has revealed to us, we refrain from making any judgments about the extent of anyone else's communication with God. Above all, we reverence the sanctity of each human person, knowing as we do the sanctification which God's love has worked in us.

Addressed as it is to the Christian community — a community which knows itself to be the sanctified, sacred Body of Christ on earth, loved by the Father as Jesus Himself is loved (see *John,* chapters 13-17; especially 14:16-23; 15:9; 16:27), this instruction of Jesus says more than the commandment of Leviticus, "You shall love your neighbor as yourself" (*Leviticus* 19:18). The teaching of Jesus presupposes a love of self based on a new appreciation, in faith, of who we are. To be consistent in our faith and true to the teachings of Jesus, we must love our own selves with the love Jesus was talking about when He said, "He who welcomes you welcomes me, and he who welcomes me welcomes him who sent me . . . I promise you that whoever gives a cup of cold water to one of these lowly ones because he is a disciple will not want for his reward" (*Matthew* 10:40-42). If we believe that anyone who welcomes a little child for Jesus' sake is welcoming Jesus Himself (*Matthew* 18:5), then we must believe this is true also of those who welcome us. The conclusion is that we must welcome our own being with joy. We are the Body of Christ. Our life is a sharing in His, and we must rejoice in it. For all our faults and shortcomings, our temptations, woundedness and malice, we are still the Body of Christ. We are one with Jesus, and we share in His goodness the way we share in His mind and heart and life.

This goodness is our own; it is what we really are. We are not commanded to love others because Jesus is good and He loves them — as if the Gospel commandment amounted to no more than, "Love me — love my dog!" No, Jesus teaches us to love others as Himself because they really have His goodness; He has shared it with them; they have become good as He is good, in spite of all the faults that still diminish that goodness in them. And the same is true of ourselves. We are not yet perfect, but we are good with the goodness of Jesus, of God Himself. Like the water mixed with wine at the Eucharistic celebration, we have taken on His taste; it is in us; it *is* us. We are, as St. Paul expresses it, an "aroma of Christ;" in us there is the "fragrance of his knowledge" (2 *Corinthians* 2:14-15).

What makes this goodness our own is the fact that we have freely accepted it. Our minds are not composed of darkness which belongs to us and light which belongs to Christ, mixed together in one understanding like oil and water which do not blend. No, we as persons are really characterized in our own being and individuality by the truth we have freely affirmed with our minds — even though this truth is only ours by the free gift of faith, by our being granted a share in the vision of truth that God Himself enjoys. We as persons *are* the choices, the stance toward others and toward God which we freely take — even though this stance is an act of love which we can only enter into by being allowed to participate by grace in God's own infinite act of loving. We are not sanctified, made holy or good the way a container is affected by what it contains (in reality, the container is not affected at all). Through our union with Jesus we are made good the way lovers are made good through their mutual gift of self to one another. As each lover becomes what the other is, so we freely and truly, by a personal act of our own, embrace the truth and the goodness Jesus shares with us. We accept it with our minds and hearts, and we become what we accept. We become one mind and heart with Him, the way the water becomes one with the wine.[3]

Seen in this perspective, the commandment, "Treat others the way you would have them treat you" is really a commandment to treat others the way we would treat Christ Himself; for this is what we are, and this is what they are by the gift of baptism. St. Paul teaches this in his letter to the Ephesians, where he instructs spouses to love and respect one another as Christ Himself. Children should recognize Christ in their parents, and even slaves in their masters. And all Christians should live and love themselves as "children of light," realizing that at one time they may have been darkness, but now they *are* light in the Lord" (see *Ephesians,* chapters 5-6).

To put it in one word, the teaching, "Treat others the way you would have them treat you" comes down to the instruction Jesus gave to His disciples at the Last Supper: "This is my commandment: love one another as I have loved you" (*John* 15:12). In this is the whole doctrine of grace.

FOOTNOTES

[1] For one of the most recent examples of this, see Vatican II's "Declaration on Religious Freedom" in THE DOCUMENTS OF VATICAN II, ed. Walter M. Abbott, S.J., (America Press, 1966). An excerpt reads: "In all his activity, a man is bound to follow his conscience faithfully, in order that he may come to God, for whom he was created. It follows that he is not to be forced to act in a manner contrary to his conscience. Nor, on the other hand, is he to be restrained from acting in accordance, especially in matters religious.

"For, of its very nature, the exercise of religion consists before all else in those internal, voluntary, and free acts whereby man sets the course of his life directly toward God. No merely human power can either command or prohibit acts of this kind" (parag. 3, p. 681).

[2] For an explanation of "baptism of desire," see WHY JESUS?, chapter five, pp. 62-69; and all of chapter six (Dimension Books, 1981).

[3] For a further development of this, see my previous book, FIRST STEPS IN CHRISTIAN DISCIPLESHIP — *The Experience of Accepting Jesus,* chapter one: "Accepting the Call to Conversion" (Dimension Books, 1982). See also WHY JESUS?, chapter four: "Jesus is Fullness of Life."

CHAPTER FOURTEEN: THE VALUE YOU RESPECT
IS THE VALUE YOU PROJECT — *Matthew* 7:12

Summary:

1. Jesus told His followers: "Treat others as you would have them treat you." This should keep the Christian community from ever taking a stance of superiority toward any other person or group. Christians should give to others — including those of other, non-Christian religions — the reverence and respect which they believe is due to themselves as the Body of Christ, children of God and temples of the Holy Spirit.

2. Christians brought human rights into focus by claiming for themselves the freedom to follow their consciences and the teaching of Jesus Christ regardless of any human prohibition. But Christians have not always allowed this same freedom of conscience to others. We recognize today that, among other things, this was a violation of Christ's commandment to treat others as we would have them treat us.

3. Jesus gave us the example of doing just this. He was God and deserved to be treated as God. But insofar as was legitimate and possible He treated us as His God, serving us and dying for us.

4. This same instruction calls upon us to love ourselves as we deserve to be loved. We are the Body of Christ, temples of His Spirit. We are one with Christ, in spite of our shortcomings.

5. Through our union with Jesus we ourselves become good. It is we who affirm with our minds and embrace with our wills the truth and goodness He shares with us through grace. In freely accepting His grace we become what we accept, and His goodness becomes truly our own.

Questions for prayer and discussion:

1. How does the awareness I have of my own value through grace affect the way I look upon others? Does it increase my reverence for them? Why? In what ways do I show a reverence for others which is inspired by my understanding of grace?

2. Do I respect the human rights of others as I would want my own to be respected? Am I as careful about the rights, the feelings, the reputation of every other person as I would want others to be about my wife, daughter, husband, son? Is this true of people I see as being on the "wrong side" — e.g., criminals, adversaries, people who propagate attitudes and values I believe are destructive? How would I apply to these situations the teaching, "Treat others as you would want to be treated?"

3. Do I in any way look down upon people of other religions? On non-Christians? On people who have not had the particular religious experience I have had or who don't seem to be as "turned on" to Jesus as I am? What damage has Christian contempt for non-believers (or for those considered less holy) done in the past? Have I ever done damage in the same way?

4. How did Jesus follow His own teaching and treat us as He Himself should have been treated? How can I follow His example in this?

5. Why should I reverence and value myself — my own being, my person — with the reverence due to Christ Himself? Should my faults prevent me from doing this? Why? Is the same true for my attitude toward others? Why?

CHAPTER FIFTEEN

THE CHOICE OF A CHANNEL OR STAR
Freedom Is An Open Sea

The next passage in the Sermon on the Mount is the last thing a scrupulous person needs to hear: "Enter through the narrow gate. The gate that leads to damnation is wide, the road is clear, and many choose to travel it. But how narrow is the gate that leads to life, how rough the road, and how few there are who find it!" (*Matthew* 7:13-14).

This passage is death for the scrupulous; and for all of us it tends to be depressing. We feel the walls closing in: "Enter through the narrow gate . . . How narrow is the gate that leads to life." The word "narrow" alone is enough to freeze our juices. Who wants a "narrow" anything, much less a religion?

The good news of this passage is that the narrowest reality man has conceived of is a straight line. In pure mathematics a straight line has no breadth at all. And for that very reason it is not constricting. One cannot be inside of a straight line; it is not a channel, but a direction-indicator: it simply points us toward a goal.

If we think of religion as a channel that we follow, a "safe" or moral area marked off and bounded by commandments on either side, then the path of our religion can be more or less broad or narrow. To make the commandments more strict is to narrow down our field of activity; it is to limit the scope of our free choice, to constrict our souls. At least, it can feel like this.

If, however, we think of our religion as a straight line which focuses us on the person of Jesus Christ as on a fixed star that we navigate by, there is no sense of constriction at all. Those who sail by the stars are not hemmed in; the whole, wide ocean is theirs.

Yet their course is the narrowest path that can be, because it is a straight line to the goal. This is what the religion of Jesus Christ is for those who look, not to the law, but to the person of Jesus as their model and rule of life (see 2 *Corinthians* 4:1-18; *Hebrews* 3:1; *Philippians* 2:5-11; 1 *Peter* 2:21-25).

To set one's sights on Jesus Himself; to aim at absorbing His mind and values, His attitudes and priorities, His ideals and goals: this is the only valid course for Christians. Our religion is not a system of rules and observances, but a religion of personal relationship with God. Morality is not what it is all about, but communion. The goal of Christian living is not sinlessness, but perfect likeness to Christ, perfect oneness with Him in mind and heart and action. Jesus came that we might have life, and have it to the full (see *John* 10:10). And this is what the fullness of life consists in: "To know you, the only true God, and him whom you have sent, Jesus Christ" (*John* 17:3).

On the one hand, this is the narrowest religion conceivable: if perfection is our path, then any deviation at all from perfect response to Christ will be off course. It will be "sin" in the Scriptural meaning of the word *(hamartia),* which is to "miss." For this reason Christians always present themselves before God and before the world as sinners. We never live up to our religion; we always fall short. To the teaching of Jesus, "You must be made perfect as your heavenly Father is perfect" (*Matthew* 5:48), the response of every Christian heart is the prayer of the man in the Gospel: "O God, be merciful to me, a sinner" (see *Luke* 18:9-14).

On the other hand, this is the most free of all religions. It carries with it the feeling of the open sea: without boundaries or restrictions, simply one fixed star to set a course by.

Freedom is not measured by the number of options one has. I have known people who were young, unmarried, and free to choose any career they wanted, but who were simply unable to make up their minds. They felt no driving motivation toward anything. As a result they described themselves as "frustrated," "boxed in," unable to move. They felt they were chained to one spot while life was passing them by. They certainly did not feel free. And yet, they had every option in the world.

Freedom consists essentially in the power to live life fully and to express without restraint the true goodness and beauty that are within us. This presupposes self control. When a dancer is able to execute with ease the intricate, difficult steps of a ballet, both the dancer and the spectators have a sense of freedom in motion. Freedom is spirit made flesh: when we are able to express perfectly with our bodies the thoughts, the feelings, the inspirations and beauty that are welling up in our souls, that is freedom. It is wholeness; it is self-integration; it is self-realization.

Perfect freedom is perfect self-expression.

Applied to religion, this means that we are perfectly free in our religion when we are able to express our true selves authentically to God. But the true self of every Christian is a covenanted self. The "I" of every Christian is an "I" united to God: this is what grace is all about. " . . . The life I live now is not my own; Christ is living in me" (*Galatians* 2:20).

St. Paul, in his writings, uses some thirty times the prefix "co-" (in Greek *syn*-) to express the intimate and mysterious union of Christians with Jesus. These words, many of them coined by Paul himself, are a characteristic of Paul's theology, and they do not translate directly into English. Thus we "co-live" with Christ, "co-suffer" with Him, were "co-crucified" with Him, "co-died" with Him in baptism and were "co-raised" with Him from the dead. We will be "co-glorified" and "co-reign" with Him, since we were "co-formed" into the pattern of His death.

St. Paul also uses 164 times the expression "in Christ" or its equivalent. This too is an expression that is characteristic of Paul's theology, and its significance is the same: Paul uses it to express the mystery of grace, which is the favor of sharing in God's own life by being incorporated into Christ, made members of His Body on earth.[1]

If the true self of a Christian is the self united to Christ, then authentic self-expression for any Christian means graced self-expression: co-expression with Christ, a response to reality which is both divine and human at the same time. In other words, perfect freedom for Christians is realized in those actions in which the Spirit of Christ finds most perfect expression. Freedom is spirit made flesh; and therefore, for us who are joined to Christ, freedom consists in letting the Spirit of God who dwells within us express Himself without restraint in and through our human actions. This is perfect surrender, perfect love and perfect freedom all identified in one act.

This is why the Christian course is at one and the same time the narrowest and the least constricting of all paths. It is the freest way and the way that allows for the least deviation. Those who understand it as a direct, unwavering thrust toward total identification with Christ can claim the "glorious freedom of the children of God" (*Romans* 8:21); they have experienced it. In changing their focus from what is lawful to what is "good, pleasing and perfect" in the sight of God, they have felt themselves released from slavery (see *Romans* 12:1-2 and 1 *Corinthians* 6:12). This is not a freedom that gives "free rein to the flesh" (*Galatians* 5:13) or encourages anyone to despise authority (see 2 *Peter* 2:10-22). It is rather a freedom found in loving surrender to the Holy Spirit who has become the inner law of the disciple's heart. "Where the Spirit of the Lord is, there is freedom" (see 2 *Corinthians* 3:1-18), because the Spirit of the Lord is the Spirit given to us, the Spirit who has become one with our own spirit. And to give one's own spirit unimpeded expression in the flesh is to be free.

Whenever a Christian community loses sight of Christ; whenever — on both the individual and the community level — personal relationship with Jesus and personal responsiveness to Him drop out of focus, then that community is launched on the wide, clear path that leads to destruction. The path may appear very narrow indeed, being a path that is essentially law-observance, bounded by rules. But no matter how narrow it is, it is wider than a straight line. It is the broad path compared to a straight course to Jesus. And the narrower it is, the clearer it will be. Rules are like that: the more they constrict our lives the simpler living becomes. A life entirely governed by rules would be a life without any decision-making at all, and there is no path to follow that could possibly be clearer than that. But it leads to destruction; it is the denial of life itself, both human and divine.

The way of Jesus is a narrow way, being a straight line. And it can be rough (see *Matthew* 7:14). But it is the way of life. It is the way of freedom, of positive self-direction, of challenge and response. It is a way that calls us beyond ourselves. And in so doing it calls us into the life of God.[2]

The first duty of the Christian community, then, is not to make its way of life clear by establishing rules. The first duty of the community is to put each and every member into contact with the lifegiving, the inspiring model of Jesus Christ. Rules have their importance; no community can express its identity without some. But rules are not the religion of Jesus because they are only channel markers. The religion of Jesus is a straight course determined by one fixed star.

FOOTNOTES

[1] See Fernand Prat, S.J., THE THEOLOGY OF SAINT PAUL, tr. John L. Stoddard, Vol. II, pp. 18-20 and 391-395. Fr. Prat lists the words in St. Paul's writings that begin with *syn-* in Greek, and tells where they are found. For those who would like to follow up the references, I have substituted English words for the Greek:

co-suffer: Romans 8:17; 1 Corinthians 12:26
co-crucified: Romans 6:6; Galatians 2:20
co-die: 2 Timothy 2:11; cf. 2 Corinthians 7:3
co-buried: Romans 6:4; Colossains 2:12
co-resurrected: Ephesians 2:6; Colossians 2:12; 3:1

co-live: Romans 6:8; 2 Timothy 2:11
co-vivified (brought to life with): Ephesians 2:5;
    Colossians 2:13
co-formed (configured): Phillippians 3:10, 21; Romans 8:21
co-glorified: Romans 8:17
co-seated: Ephesians 2:6
co-reign: 2 Timothy 2:12; cf. 1 Corinthians 4:8
co-planted: Romans 6:5
co-inheritor: Romans 8:17; Ephesians 3:6
co-sharer: Ephesians 3:6; 5:7
co-embodied: Ephesians 3:6
co-built: Ephesians 2:22
co-structured: (and connected) Ephesians 2:21;
    Ephesians 4:16; Colossians 2:19

[2] For a development of the idea that Christianity is a way of growth precisely through challenging us to live on the divine level of perfect faith, hope and love, see WHY JESUS?, chapters seven to ten.

CHAPTER FIFTEEN: THE CHOICE OF A CHANNEL OR STAR — *Matthew* 7:13-14

Summary:

1. The religion of Jesus is not a channel bounded by commandments which make it narrower or broader according to how strict they are. Jesus teaches us to set our course by focusing on His own person, as on a fixed star. His is not a religion of rules and observances, but of personal relationship. This makes it at one and the same time the freest and the narrowest of all religions. The course it calls for is a straight line to the ideal of perfection itself, which is to live according to the mind and heart of Jesus.

2. Christianity's emphasis is not on negative rules and commandments, but on positive response to the "fullness of life" held up to us by Jesus. Therefore the followers of Jesus should not feel hemmed in or constricted by their religion. On the other hand, since no one ever lives up to the ideal perfectly, but everyone "misses the mark" to some degree, Christians always see themselves as sinners. This is not a source of guilt and anxiety, but it should keep us in an attitude of peaceful humility and gratefulness before God and men.

3. Freedom consists essentially in the power to live life fully, and to express one's most authentic self without restraint.

Perfect freedom is perfect self-expression. Self-control is not opposed to this but presupposed, as in a dancer. As Christians we are most free when our true — our graced — selves are able to express themselves most fully in our actions.

4. The true self of a Christian is the self united to Christ. It is "in Christ" and with Him and through Him that we express ourselves most authentically to the Father. In us and with us and through us Christ continues to express Himself to the world. Thus we "co-live" and "co-act" with Christ, just as through baptism we "co-died" and "co-rose" with Him. For us, to be free is to be surrendered entirely to the action of Jesus within us. Perfect freedom for Christians is realized in those actions in which the Spirit of Jesus finds most perfect expression. Freedom is Spirit made flesh.

Questions for prayer and discussion:

1. Do I experience my religion as constricting? As oppressive? As a source of anxiety? How much do I focus on its rules and obligations, and how much on the positive, inspiring ideals of Jesus Christ? Is my primary goal to "keep in bounds" or to live in all of its fulness the life held out to me by Jesus? In what concrete ways do I, in my life, experience myself as living by the ideals of Jesus rather than by a set of laws?

2. When I say, "Lord, have mercy on me a sinner," do I say this because of specific sins against the commandments, or because I see how, in very specific ways, I am falling short of the ideals preached by Jesus? If to "sin" is to "miss the mark," should every sin cause me to feel guilt and anxiety? Why? What is the "mark" for Christians?

3. How would I define freedom? What image best expresses this definition to me? What do I think of the image of the dancer used in this chapter? What does it say to me about freedom?

4. Would I agree that Christians are most free when they are most surrendered to Christ and to the action of Christ's Spirit within them? Why? When do I experience myself as most free? When do I feel I am being most authentically myself?

CHAPTER SIXTEEN

ONLY THE LIVE CAN TEACH
A Duty to Look for the Spirit

How is the Christian community to know whether or not its life is on course? If the community is living with the "glorious freedom of the children of God" proclaimed by St. Paul (*Romans* 8:21) — that is, if it tries to set its course by the fixed star, which is Jesus, and by the inspirations of the Holy Spirit in its midst instead of by the channel-markers of the law (which are clear and unchanging precisely because they are dead) — what is to preserve it from illusion?

The problem is not that Jesus changes while the law does not. The same word of God which urges us to embrace our Christian freedom also warns us against being "carried away by all kinds of strange teaching." "Jesus Christ," we are told, "is the same yesterday, today, and forever" (see *Hebrews* 13:9). And if the law of God is eternal, so are the words of Jesus. "The heavens and the earth will pass away," He tells us, "but my words will not pass" (*Mark* 13:31; see also *Luke* 16:17; *John* 12:47-48; 13:23-26; 15:7; *Revelation* 22:18-19).

As we have seen, however, the words of Jesus teach us principles; they do not, as a rule, translate directly into detailed and practical laws (see above, chapters two and fifteen). And since a principle is that from which something begins, it is to be expected that the words of Jesus will generate, not terminate, discussion and debates within the Christian community. Where the community is alive, there will be disagreements to settle. Wherever the Spirit is not stifled (see 1 *Thessalonians* 5:19-20), there will be prophecies true and false to evalute (see 1 *Corinthians* 14:29). What criterion shall the community use to judge whether or not a given inspiration is from the Spirit of God?

We have already seen (chapter twelve) how the early Church decided questions of this kind. They used their intellects in rational dialogue to apply the objective truth of Scripture and the subjective, spiritual experience of the community (and of individuals) to the problem at hand. And the decision of the community was authoritative: "It is the decision of the Holy Spirit, and ours too," wrote the participants in the first Council of the Church "not to lay on you any burden beyond that which is strictly necessary . . . " (see *Acts* 15:28).

In the Sermon on the Mount Jesus introduces another element that should be taken into consideration: the spiritual life of the person who is speaking. "Be on your guard against false prophets . . . " He warns. "Do you ever pick grapes from thornbushes, or figs from prickly plants?" (*Matthew* 7:15-16).

Ours is an age of professionalism. There is a tendency to presume that anyone with an academic degree in theology is qualified to teach in the Church. As an extreme (and rare) example of this, some church-affiliated universities have retained atheists as theology professors on the grounds that one does not have to believe what one is teaching in order to teach it well. Another example is book publishing: like every business, it tends to be ruled by the market, with the result that editors may find themselves looking more toward possible sales than they do at the source of a manuscript. The ruling question can become, not "What spirit inspired this writing?" but "How many readers will it appeal to?" Religion textbooks on the grade school and high school levels are a big business, and big business methods are used to sell them — which means that profits and sales promotion have a lot to do with what is actually taught in the schools. The media industry is yoked even more closely to profits: any priest, minister or prophet who can attract a large enough audience is certain to get into print, onto the air, or into a television program. This is the world as it is, and there is no simple way to change it.

The solution does not lie in simplistic efforts at censorship. Nor can those who choose religion teachers, directors of religious education or textbooks for use in the schools form themselves into vigilante committees to spy out the morals of the people they deal with. And yet, if the instruction of Jesus about false prophets means anything at all, there must be efforts at discernment. Every Christian community must exercise some spiritual discretion in its choice of the teachers it will listen to and entrust with the formation of its young.

The instruction of Jesus is that we should look for positive signs of God's life in those who would teach us His way. "By their fruits you will know them . . . You can tell a tree by its fruit" (see *Matthew* 7:16-20).

Morality is not a sign of God's life. At least, in itself it is not a clear sign. It is possible, theoretically, at least, to be quite moral without living the life of grace at all. It may not be very likely; and some distinctions might be called for in the meaning we give to "moral," but a good, ordinary life without notice-able acts of "sin" is no proof that one is living the life of God. Jesus said to His disciples about the Pharisees, whose lives reeked with morality, "I tell you, unless your holiness surpasses that of the scribes and Pharisees you shall not enter the kingdom of God" (*Matthew* 5:20). Jesus' whole teaching in the Sermon on the Mount is an instruction on how to go beyond morality.

Anyone accepted as a teacher in the Church should show positive signs of a spiritual life that goes beyond good behavior — a way of living which can only be explained and understood as inspired by deep faith, motivated by a hope which reaches beyond the rewards of life on this earth, and characterized by a love which is more than human. The graced life, the authentically Christian life, is a sharing in the life of God; and only those can effectively teach this life whose own way of acting is inexplicable without the indwelling presence of God in their hearts.

We are tempted to make a distinction between those teachers who simply pass on the doctrine commonly accepted in the community and those who have something original to offer. And it is true that for the second kind more scrutiny is needed. But no one can even teach a child to say the Our Father as it should be said unless the teacher vibrates to that prayer in his or her own heart. Authentic teaching is one tenth instruction and nine tenths inspiration. Especially is this true of religion: to teach faith, hope and love is to communicate one's own spirit to others. And to teach any Christian doctrine in a way that is not at the same time and inseparably an inspiration to faith, hope and love is to pass off dead wood for a forest. Jesus was not an academic teacher; His doctrine is not an academic doctrine; and to present it in a way that does not stir the heart is to falsify the word and the message of Christ.

But only what comes from the heart can stir the heart. "Do you ever pick grapes from thornbushes, or figs from prickly plants?" Or does live fruit grow on dead wood? Jesus came to "light a fire on earth" (*Luke* 12:49) and only those can help to kindle it whose hearts are burning within them (see *Luke* 24:32).

Before accepting any teacher, then — and not just those whose doctrine is controversial — the Christian community should look for positive signs of a fervent spiritual life in those who present themselves.

A "spiritual life" is a life lived by the Spirit of God. It is not just a life of law observance or of routine Christianity. It is a life characterized by the gifts of the Spirit — wisdom, understanding, knowledge, counsel, fortitude, piety, fear of the Lord (see *Isaiah* 11:2). And it accredits itself by the "fruit of the Spirit: love, joy, peace, patient endurance, kindness, generosity, faith, mildness and chastity" (see *Galatians* 5:22-23).

I have filled out many a questionnaire sent to me by establishments to whom my name had been given as a reference by some prospective employee. I have been asked to rate friends and colleagues according to a scale of ten for dependability, initiative, professional talent, ability to work harmoniously with others. I have never been asked, however, to testify to the "fruit of the Spirit" — to say what I have seen and felt in my friends of love, joy, peace, patient endurance, kindness, generosity, faith, gentleness and self-control. Yet I find these qualities at least as observable as others I have been asked to make judgments on.

The "fruit of the Spirit" — real evidence of a spiritual life — is not to be sought in impressive accomplishments. "None of those," Jesus says, "who cry out 'Lord, Lord' will enter the kingdom of God, but only the one who does the will of my Father in heaven" (*Matthew* 7:21). As we have seen, to do the Father's will as a Christian means more than keeping the commandments; it means response to the Spirit of God. A theologian can say "Lord, Lord" and expound on the meaning of the word with intellectual brilliance so as to astound both men and angels. This may impress audiences. But unless the Spirit in his heart is crying out "Abba! Father!" with love, he is but a "noisy gong, a clanging cymbal" (see 2 *Corinthians* 13:1; *Romans* 8:15; *Galatians* 4:6). There are people with great insight into the spirit of the times, who can stir hearts as prophets of the culture. They can sense the needs of people and exorcise the demons of confusion, discouragement and apathy, working wonders of psychological healing, all in the name of religion. Yet Jesus says of them, "When that day comes, many will plead with me, 'Lord, Lord, have we not prophesied in your name? Have we not exorcised demons by its power? Did we not do many miracles in your name as well?' Then I will declare to them solemnly, 'I never knew you. Out of my sight, you evildoers!'" (*Matthew* 7:22-23Y: see also 1 *Corinthians* 13:2-3).

By their fruits you shall know them — not by their results. Results can be deceptive; they can proceed from too many causes to be a sure sign of the Spirit of God. If apostolic fruitfulness is measured by results — by the number of converts, the enthusiasm of one's hearers, or even by the obedience one's followers give to everything that is asked of them, then some of the most apostolically fruitful individuals on earth have been leaders of cults. The Rev. Jim Jones, whose followers mass-murdered themselves, one another and their children in Guyana was such a charismatic leader. So was Adolf Hitler. And on a much less destructive level, so are the popular evangelists whose vaudeville antics on TV are only less disgraceful than the huckster pitch for money which punctuates their every program.

Of more real concern to us, however, should be the quite legitimate preachers, teachers and interpreters of Christianity whose doctrine is both serious and sophisticated, but who are popular with people precisely because they tell them what they want to hear. Those who keep recycling the *status quo* are exalted by the conservatives as defenders of the faith, while those who have the eloquence to put teeth marks on the establishment are held up by the liberals as prophets. There is no apostolic fruitfulness in selling phariseeism to the pharisees and anarchy to the anarchists. But the fastest way to get a following is to become the prophet of some particular faction's party line. On a campus stress the social teachings of the Church but preach enlightened laxity with regard to sex. To the older, moneyed class, however, insist on premarital chastity for the young and play down the radicalism of Christian teaching on peace and justice. Among intellectuals take an attitude of superiority toward dogma and be silent about devotion. With the superstitious insist on faith. Preachers and teachers who are perceptive enough to do this will always find a following. But they are false prophets. Of such people we might say, "By their results you will know what they are not."

A true prophet is known, not by his visible success, but by the evidence of grace in his own spiritual life. And this grace should appear, not just in his private, personal life, but in the apostolate, which is, in any authentic minister, the public face of his soul. The "spiritual life" is not just private; it is the life of the Spirit manifesting itself in everything one does. If in the preaching and writing of any minister there is not something that proclaims, "Be imitators of me, as I am of Christ," that minister is without accreditation as a prophet.[1]

A Christian community is a community guided, not by laws, but by the living Spirit of Jesus, the Holy Spirit who dwells and speaks within the community, enlightening and empowering it to live on the level of God's own life. For this reason those who guide the community, teach it, inspire it and determine its course of action must be men and women of the Spirit. And the community has a responsibility to discern whether or not the lives of those who would be its teachers are really spiritual lives, lives of response to the Spirit.

To some this may sound like an unrealistic undertaking. But which is more unrealistic: to try to determine who lives by the Spirit of God, or to hope that someone who does not will be able to communicate the spirit of Christ to others? Christianity is by its very nature an unrealistic undertaking; it is a level of life and activity possible only to God. Only those who share in the life of God and participate in the nature of God through incorporation into Christ can perform the slightest act on the level of Christian faith, hope and love. Therefore all is gift. The power to discern the presence (or absence) of the Spirit in those who address the community is no less and no more a free gift of God than the gift of grace itself (see 1 *Corinthians* 12:10). For that reason the community which believes and professes that grace is its very life must also believe and profess that the grace of discernment which is necessary to maintain its life will also be given to it.

The community declares its faith in this by the simple act of trying to discern. And this act, like every other effort of human beings to cooperate with grace, will sometimes end in failure. But even failure is a witness to belief. Only those can fail who believe enough to try.

FOOTNOTE

[1] See 1 *Corinthians* 11:1. St. Paul says this repeatedly of himself. See 1 *Corinthians* 4:16; *Philippians* 3:17; 1 *Thessalonians* 1:6; 2 *Thessalonians* 3:7. See also 1 *Corinthians* 2:1-16; 4:9-13; 2 *Corinthians* 2:14-17 and chapters 10-13.

CHAPTER SIXTEEN: ONLY THE LIVE CAN TEACH —
Matthew 7:15-23

Summary:

1. In a community which lives by the Spirit rather than by the law, and by prophetic inspirations rather than by dead conformity, both true and false prophets are bound to emerge. We have seen three criteria of discernment taught in the Scriptures: reason, Scripture and spiritual experiences. Jesus here proposes a fourth: the spiritual life of the person who is speaking.
2. There is a tendency to presume that professional training qualifies a person to minister in the Church. A reason for this may be that it is fairly easy to measure a person's professional competence. It is much harder to discern whether or not someone is leading an authentically spiritual life. And yet, the fruit a person bears in the apostolate of the Church

depends more on union with God than on professional or academic training. A Christian community, then, must look for signs of authentic spiritual life and experience in one who is to be entrusted with a teaching or pastoral function in the community.

3. A "spiritual life" is more than a moral life; more than morally irreproachable behavior. Anyone accepted for ministry in the Church should show positive signs of a life characterized by deep faith, eschatalogical hope, and graced, enduring love. Candidates for ministry should be evaluated in terms of the way the gifts and fruits of the Holy Spirit appear in their lives.

4. To judge a life by its fruits is not the same as judging it by its accomplishments. Many people achieve impressive results on the human and psychological level — results which remove the obstacles to conversion of mind, heart and behavior — without themselves being significantly surrendered to God. A true prophet is known by the evidence of grace in his or her own spiritual life. And the working of this grace should appear unambiguously in the apostolate.

Questions for prayer and reflection:

1. Who exercises the "prophetic" function in the Church today? Are theologians, teachers, pastoral ministers, writers, etc. ever sources of dissension in the Church? What criteria do I apply in order to distinguish between true and false prophets? What criteria does my Christian community apply?

2. What is the role of professional training in a Church ministry? Would it discourage people from getting professional training if Church communities insisted on deep spirituality in their ministers and teachers? Are spirituality and professionalism incompatible? Which, in my opinion, is emphasized more in the formation and selection of Church teachers and ministers today? What do I see as the fruit of this?

3. Who do I know who has a deep and authentic spiritual life? What signs reveal this to me? What signs of a spiritual life could I look for with some hope of identifying them in a person previously unknown to me? Do I think the gifts and fruits of the Spirit could be used as criteria in evaluating candidates for positions in Church ministry?

4. What "fruit of the Spirit" can I identify in my own life? What fruit seems to be missing? Is my life characterized by love, joy, peace, patient endurance, kindness, generosity, faith, gentleness and self-control? Is this true at home, at work, in my social life?

CHAPTER SEVENTEEN

UNDERSTANDING IS WITH THE HEART
Do and You Shall Know

There is only one sure proof of belief; and that is to act on what one believes. And so Jesus concludes His Sermon on the Mount with the declaration: "Anyone who hears my words and puts them into practice is like the wise man who built his house on rock . . . Anyone who hears my words and does not put them into practice is like the foolish man who built his house on sandy ground . . . " (see *Matthew* 7:24-27).

Jesus is a teacher of life. Only those who study His words in order to live by them are truly His disciples. To study Jesus' words in any other way is to guarantee distortion — like trying to make artwork out of blueprints. Jesus is the "Master of the Way," and only those who follow Him have any hope of grasping what He teaches.

Authentic discipleship, therefore, is not a journey of the head. It is a journey of the heart. Those who do not listen to Jesus with wills poised to respond and to carry out His teaching into action are listening with deaf ears. Jesus Himself quoted Isaiah to this effect:

> "Listen as you will, you shall not understand, look
> intently as you will, you shall not see. Sluggish indeed
> is this people's heart . . .
>
>   (*Matthew* 13:14-15; see *Isaiah* 6:9-10).

St. Paul made a distinction between the wisdom
that can be taught to the "spiritually mature" and the
instruction those are only ready to receive who are
still "infants in Christ" (see 1 *Corinthians* 2:6; 3:1).
The difference between the two groups is not determined by intellectual capacity or by education; the
key element is readiness of heart. The words of Jesus
are unintelligible to us until we are ready to live them.

This is why there is no such thing as an authentically Christian study group, church community,
parish or discussion club unless its members are
seriously bent on changing their lifestyle. Conversion
is the name of the game, from the beginning of our
encounter with Jesus until the day we meet Him face-
to-face at death and surrender our hearts entirely to
Him in love.[1]

Jesus is a way of life, and life is the surest sign we
have that we are in His way. A Christian community
which cannot lead its members into the experience of
new life, the life Christ promised to give, will never
retain them. Or if it does, it will retain them, not as
disciples, but as the reality it has become itself:
dead wood.

The sign of new life is deceptive, however. False
prophets hold up the promise of new life, and those
who follow them feel they are coming alive. This is
because any increase of vitality — of enthusiasm, joy,
motivation, hope, or relationship with others — is an
increase of life on some level. It is new life; it is just
not necessarily the life Jesus came to give.

The life Christ came to give is not just new the way fresh leaves on a tree are new: a new outcropping or augmentation of what is basically the same old thing. Leaves in the springtime are exciting, but they are not really new. We have seen them before. And the enthusiasm engendered by the "bubble groups" in and outside of Christianity — the sects and cults and community churches, the rootless religions and one-building denominations which depend for their existence on the personality of the preacher or the contagious involvement of the congregation — these are not new either. They are a repetition of the ages-old phenomenon of religious enthusiasm. They do give new life; but the life they give is indistinguishable in its nature and effects from the very positive (and sometimes very negative) consequences of a psychological high. Divine life may be working within these experiences, because God is not stingy with redemption, and the grace of Christ flows sometimes through the strangest of channels (see WHY JESUS?, chapter six: "Jesus Is An Inescapable Question"). But what we commonly observe appears to be essentially a new level, a new intensity, of more wholesome human life, animated in greater or lesser degree by the Gospel, depending on the group, and undoubtedly aided by grace.[2]

The new life of Christ is more than this. It is something new to creation itself. It is a "new thing on earth" (see *Jeremiah* 31:22, 31-34; *Ezekiel* 11:19; 36:23-28; *Isaiah* 43:19; *Matthew* 9:17). It is the life of God which came to earth in Jesus at the Incarnation and has been passed down through the ages to all those who by baptism have become one with Christ, one Body with Him. The new life of Christ is Jesus' own life, the life proper to Him as Incarnate Son of God. It is a life that is uniquely His, and He cannot share it in its authentic fullness with anyone except by uniting them to Himself as members of His Body: members united with the head, branches grafted on to the vine.

The new life of Christ is the life of His Body on earth. It is the life of the Christian community, the life which the Body draws from Jesus who is its head, and from the Spirit of Jesus, who is its very soul. And all of the members contribute to the upbuilding of this life in one another. This is what Christian discipleship is all about. As St. Paul puts it: "Let us profess the truth in love and *grow* to the full maturity of Christ the head." Growth in union with Christ, growth in His life, is what Christian community is all about: "Through him the whole body grows, and with the proper functioning of the members joined firmly together by each supporting ligament, builds itself up in love" (*Ephesians* 4:15-16; see also 2:20-22).

To grow in Christ's life is to grow in union with Him and with one another. The direction of Christ's activity on earth — of all graced action — is toward the unity and reconciliation of every human spirit in the one Body of Christ: "to bring all things in the heavens and on earth into one under Christ's headship" (*Ephesians* 1:10).

Divisions exist in Christianity, sad divisions which grew out of human sins and errors which were active on both sides every time the Body split again. In our day the wounds have not healed, but disciples are looking toward healing. The fragmentation of Christianity is recognized for what it is: a proof of the sinfulness which in every age and in every human heart works against the unifying, reconciling, reforming action of Jesus the head and of His Spirit. The action of Jesus is always toward unity: that was and is still His mission on earth (see 2 *Corinthians* 5:16-21; *Ephesians* 1:9-10; 2:11-22; 4:1-16; *Colossians* 1:15-23; *John* 17:13-23). One sign, therefore, that a person or group is living by the life of Christ is concern for the unity of the whole Body. Groups that are comfortable in their separateness from the rest of the community of believers are shown to be in that same measure separate from the Spirit of Christ. The disciples of Jesus are instinctively drawn to form a single body with one another, for that is what they are.

The new life of Jesus, therefore, is not to be simplistically identified with those groups whose freshness and enthusiasm make them appear most visibly alive. On the other hand, where there is no freshness and enthusiasm, where the gifts and fruits of the Holy Spirit are not manifest, where the community of believers do not unmistakably love one another, and are not growing in wisdom and understanding, then no matter how orthodox the community's doctrine may be, or how undeviating its way, it will wither. The way and the truth of the Christian community are only made credible in its life. What people ask from a religion, and what Jesus taught us we should ask, is not truth in the abstract, but truth that leads to life. And it seems to be a law of religious history that whenever a community, a teacher or a guru is able to give people the experience of life on a higher or deeper level, those who perceive their lives to be enriched will not be very critical of the doctrine or morality that is taught. People will accept almost any way and any truth so long as it gives them new life. That is why Jesus proclaimed Himself, and we must present Him to the world, as "the way, and the truth, and the life" (*John* 14:6).

A Christian community can build itself on orthodoxy, making its security consist in keeping the doctrine of Jesus unchanged. If it bases its security on that alone, it is building on sand. It can base its life on morality, adhering rigidly to the straight path of precepts and commands. Still it is building on sand. It can even base its life on sophisticated discussions of the Gospel and make Scripture the focal point of its intellectual growth. But when "the rains fall, the torrents come and the winds blow" it will collapse (see *Matthew* 7:27). The only valid ground on which to build a Christian community is Christ's word carried out into action. And this means prophetic witness.

The last words Matthew writes in connection with the Sermon on the Mount are: "When Jesus finished this discourse, the crowds were spellbound. The reason was that he taught with authority and not like their own teachers" (see *Matthew* 7:28-29).

This leaves us with a decision to make. It is a faith decision. We must make it both as individuals and as a community. The question we must answer is, "Do I — and do we — believe that Jesus Christ is the way, the truth, and the life? If so, am I willing — and are we willing as a community — to base our whole lives on His teaching?"

This doesn't mean, "Are we willing to follow His laws?" It means are we willing to accept Him as "Master of the Way," as the Teacher of Life, as the one whose word, whose example, and whose way gives life to everything we do: at home, at work, in our social lives, in our civic involvement and political options, in every free and rational decision that determines the course and tone of our existence? Are we willing — and decided — to be His disciples? To search out His attitudes and values? To apply them to the concrete, practical realities of our own lives? To listen for the word which God is speaking to us now through the Scriptures, and the word which He is speaking to us through the Spirit who dwells in our midst, and to follow this word in faith, in hope and in love? Are we decided, both individually and as a community — as a family, a group of friends, as a parish or a church — to be His disciples?

If we are so decided, then the rest of our lives will be a journey into living like God.

FOOTNOTES

[1] See *Matthew* 3:2 and 4:17. This theme is developed in my first book on discipleship, which deals with the nature and experience of conversion and some of its basic content. See FIRST STEPS IN CHRISTIAN DISCIPLESHIP: *The Experience of Accepting Jesus* (Dimension Books, 1982), especially chapters one and seven: "Accepting the Call to Conversion" and "Accepting Choices As the Expression of Response." See also *His Way,* chapters 5 and 6 (St. Anthony Messenger Press, 1977).

[2] For a more developed explanation of the difference between infancy, youth and maturity in the spiritual life, see my book LIFT UP YOUR EYES TO THE MOUNTAIN, especially chapters three, four and six (Dimension Books, 1981).

CHAPTER SEVENTEEN: UNDERSTANDING IS WITH THE HEART — *Matthew* 7:24-29

Summary:

1. "In the eyes of God," someone said, "our words have only the value of our actions." Action is the only sure proof of belief. Jesus is a teacher of life, not of abstract ideas. And so only those are truly His disciples who study His words in order to live by them. The more we reflect on Christ's words without any intention of putting them into practice, the more we will distort them and the less we will understand.

2. The distinction St. Paul makes between the "spiritually mature" and those who are still "infants in Christ" is based, not on intelligence or learning, but on the willingness one has to live by the words of Christ. Discipleship matures through progressive conversion of attitudes, values and behavior. Thus there is no authentically Christian study group, Church community, parish or discussion club unless its members are seriously bent on changing their lifestyle. Continual conversion is the name of the game.

3. What attracts and holds the members of a Church congregation is the consciousness of receiving new life. This is not to be identified — although it often mistakenly is — with just any heightening of enthusiasm, motivation, or sense of relationship with others. The new life Jesus gives is new to creation itself, a "new thing on earth." It is a sharing in the life of God, and it should not be confused with just a human or psychological "high." But it needs to be experienced for the words of Jesus to retain their credibility.

4. The new life Jesus gives — shared life with God — is the life of Christ's Body on earth, the Church. Authentic growth in Christ's life, therefore, is growth into greater union with Him and with other believers. Thus a movement toward separateness from other Christians is not likely to be a movement of grace. Jesus came to draw all things together into one.

5. A Christian community can base itself and its stability on doctrine, on morality, on the beauty of its services, etc. All these are ways to build on sand. The only valid ground on which to build a Christian community is Christ's word carried out into action. This calls for discipleship and for prophetic witness. Christianity is a way of life. It must be studied as a way through reflection on Christ's words and lived as a life through choices. Authentic discipleship is a way of life and growth.

Questions for prayer and discussion:

1. What is the difference between hearing Christ's words and hearing them with a serious intention to live them out completely? Have I experienced the difference? Is it possible for a group to discuss the Scriptures with slight intention of living by them? What happens to the discussion in such a case? Could this also be the factor which makes personal meditation alive or dead?

2. Physical maturity is marked by the ability to reproduce, to give life. The passage from childhood to mature membership in society is made when one begins to contribute to society,

to work. When does a Christian become mature in the spiritual life? When is one ready to pass from children's food to an adult diet in discipleship? Have I made that passage? What are the signs of it?

3. What is the difference between the deep, solid new life of Christ and the immature enthusiasm of the various "bubble groups" who seem to bring people's lives to a new level? Can this same immaturity exist in a more established and less enthusiastic group of Christians? How? If emotion is not the key to the experience of new life in Christ, what is? Have I myself experienced the Church as bringing me to new life? How?

4. What are the signs of an authentic Church community? Would the same things be signs of authentic discipleship on the individual, personal level? Do I find these signs in my own life? In the life of my Christian community? What can I do to make both my life and that of my community more authentically a way of growth in the new life of Christ?

EPILOGUE:

HAS THE WAY BEEN TRUTH AND LIFE?

This is the third book I have written on the spiritual life using Matthew's Gospel as a guide. These books, taken together, present what I see as the first call or challenge of Matthew's Gospel and of the Christian life as such; namely, the invitation to *accept Jesus* as the saving presence of God on earth. This invitation is presented in chapters one to nine of Matthew.

The call to accept Jesus, however, is a double one. First, it is a call to accept Jesus as Savior. This call is *evangelization*. When we deeply believe that only through relationship with Jesus Christ can our existence on this earth be truly "saved" — truly redeemed from destructiveness, distortion and meaninglessness and brought to its authentic fullness both of nature and of grace — then we have been "evangelized." We have heard the good news.

The call to accept Jesus as Savior is presented most explicitly in the first two chapters of Matthew's Gospel, and these chapters (with eight and nine) provide the content for the first book in this series:

Questions for Today: WHY JESUS? This book invites us to base our whole lives on relationship — that is, on *interaction* — with Jesus as "Emmanuel", as God present to us in human ways. The choice to do this is what I would call the basic decision to be a *Christian.* WHY JESUS? talks about why we should make this decision, and what relationship with Jesus entails for us.

The second book of this series — FIRST STEPS IN CHRISTIAN DISCIPLESHIP — focuses more explicitly on Jesus as the light of the world; as Teacher of Life and "Master of the Way." In this book we are invited to be *disciples;* that is, *students* of the mind and heart of Christ. This is a second step and a deeper stage of commitment in our decision to live the Christian life.

A disciple is not just a follower. The word "disciple" means "student;" and anyone who simply walks along the way of Jesus, following obediently in His footsteps without trying to understand His mind and heart, is not truly a disciple. Such a person will not, as a matter of fact, walk in the footsteps of Jesus very long. His way of life will soon become indistinguishable — if indeed it ever differed — from the "beaten path" of his culture. If such a person's culture happens to be somewhat Christian — that is, influenced by Christian values and ideals — then the person's own life will be somewhat according to the pattern taught by Jesus. But this is not enough for a disciple.

A disciple is one who has undergone a profound conversion, not just to Jesus as Savior, but also to Jesus as "Master of the Way." A disciple believes that Jesus is the Teacher of Life — not just of "religion" in a narrow sense, but of all life. A disciple believes that the teachings of Jesus will enrich his whole existence — his family life, social life, business or professional activity, his civic and political involvement — if only he can bring each one of these areas of his living under Christ's clarifying light. The disciple does not see Jesus as the rulegiver whose message is restrictive of life. The disciple's basic act of faith is that anything and everything Jesus teaches will make his life more meaningful, more satisfying, and more productive of real joy and development, if only he can learn how to apply Christ's words to the day-to-day decisions of ordinary living. The disciple wants to know more, not less, about the message of Jesus. And he is committed to learn.

Discipleship is commitment. It is a deeper step into the total commitment of being a Christian and living a Christian life. The second and third books of this series — FIRST STEPS IN CHRISTIAN DISCIPLESHIP and MAKE ME A SABBATH OF YOUR HEART — deal with discipleship.

As I finish writing this book my thoughts turn to you, the reader, as you finish reading it. How, in fact, has it helped you?

Some readers, I hope, have not simply read this book, but have prayed their way through it. I hope that many have gathered together with friends or fellow believers to discuss the thoughts and challenges of each chapter; to share with each other the reactions and responses of their hearts; to clarify what the book has left vague; to correct anything my own commentary may have distorted; to make applications to their lives. I hope, in short, that reading this book has been an *experience* in discipleship. I hope that through this book the mind and heart of Jesus Christ has become a little more clear, a little more challenging, a little more inspiring to you. I hope above all that His words have been shown to have relevance for human life on earth today, for the life you are leading, for the decisions you are called upon to make. I hope His words have summoned you to choices, and that you have had the courage to make some.

If so, then I have the further hope that through these particular acts of "conversion" you have grown in experience of God. I hope that through each individual choice which you have made to carry Christ's teaching into action — and through the accumulation of these choices, many of which may have appeared too small to be significant — you have experienced in your life an increase, a greater and more personal appropriation of that "fullness of life" which Jesus came to give (see *John* 10:10).

If that hope has been realized, then you have already experienced the strongest motivation there is to be a disciple. You already have in your mouth the taste of what it is to be the "salt of the earth," be the measure still ever so small. If you have found light in the Gospel to clarify your attitudes toward life, then you are able to speak from personal experience of Jesus as the Light of the World and "Master of the Way." You can bear witness with St. John to a Jesus you have seen and heard and felt (see 1 *John* 1:1).

If you have experienced Jesus as the Life, then I have hope that you will continue to study Him as the Truth and to follow Him as the Way. And this is what it means to be a disciple.

APPENDIX I

METHOD OF PRAYING OVER
THE TEN COMMANDMENTS
According to St. Ignatius of Loyola

FIRST STEP:
> Take a minute or two to relax, turn off all other pre-occupations, and just recall that you are in the presence of God, that you want to spend time with Him in prayer, and that He will be with you.

SECOND STEP:
> Say a prayer asking God to help you see the Commandments from His point of view, appreciating the attitudes and values that inspired them, so that you might see how they apply to your life, and how you might live in the spirit of them perfectly.

THIRD STEP:
> Recite the First Commandment to yourself (you will find the Commandments listed in *Exodus* 20:1-17 if you don't know them by heart). Then for approximately one minute, think about this Commandment: what it means; what its real goal is and the spirit behind it; how well you have observed it; how you could observe it better.

FOURTH STEP:
> Say a short prayer to God, perhaps asking forgiveness for times and ways you failed to observe the Commandment; perhaps asking help or promising to observe it better. Say an *Our Father.*

> CONTINUE THIS WAY THROUGH ALL TEN OF THE COMMANDMENTS, OR AS MANY AS YOU WISH TO CONSIDER.

THEN:

FIFTH STEP:
> Close your prayer time with a short prayer in your own words, saying to God whatever is appropriate in the light of what has come up during the prayer time.

Note:
1. You can spend more or less time on any one Commandment, according to how much help you are getting from it.
2. This method of prayer can be used in other ways; for example, on:
   — the seven Beatitudes (*Matthew* 5:3-12)

— the Fruits of the Holy Spirit (*Galatians* 5:22-23)
— the three powers of the soul (memory, intellect, will)
— the five senses of the body
— the four cardinal moral virtues (prudence, temperance, justice, fortitude)
— the three theological virtues (faith, hope, love)
— the seven capital sins (pride, avarice, lust, anger, gluttony, envy, sloth) and the virtues opposed to them.

APPENDIX II

A METHOD FOR PRAYING OVER THE OUR FATHER
— or any other vocal prayer —

According to St. Ignatius of Loyola

FIRST STEP:

Take a minute or two to *relax,* in whatever body-position you find most helpful — walking, sitting, prostrate, or whatever. *Clear your mind* and heart of preoccupations, distractions, worries. Make yourself consciously aware that *God is present,* and that you wish to encounter Him in prayer. *Acknowledge His presence* through some physical gesture of respect: bowing, change of body-position, putting your hand on your heart, or making some other gesture according to your taste.

SECOND STEP:

Speak in your own words to the person to whom the vocal prayer is addressed (e.g., to God the Father, speaking to Him as Father) asking the grace to understand and appreciate better the prayer you are about to reflect on, and to let everything it expresses become more deeply a part of your life.

THIRD STEP:

Say the first word or phrase of the prayer (e.g., "Father" or "Our Father," or just "Our") and contemplate its meaning, i.e., reflect on it as long as you find various meanings, comparisons, insights, devotion, or inspiration through thinking about it. Then go to the next word. Do this for whatever length of time you have decided to spend in prayer.

Suggestions:

1. Do this kneeling, sitting, or in whatever position you find most helpful and most suitable to yourself.
2. During your prayer either close your eyes or keep them fixed in one position, but don't be looking around.

3. Stay on one word as long as you find in it matter for thought, devotion, or inspiration. Don't be concerned about getting through all the words. It's fine if you spend your whole time of prayer on one or two words.

4. When the time you have set for your prayer is up, say the rest of the prayer you are meditating on in the ordinary way (i.e., just reciting it), and close, if you wish, with one or another favorite vocal prayer.

5. If you spend all of your prayer one day on one or two words of the prayer, you might, on another day, say those words in the ordinary way and begin meditating on the words that come next.

FOURTH STEP:

At the end of your prayer time, turn to the person to whom the prayer is directed and in a few words thank Him and ask for the virtues or graces you see you need most.

Note:
This method can be used to pray over any vocal prayer — e.g., the *Creed* ("I believe in God . . . "); or parts of the *Eucharistic Liturgy* or *rituals,* such as the ceremony of Baptism, the Marriage rite, etc.